GDP

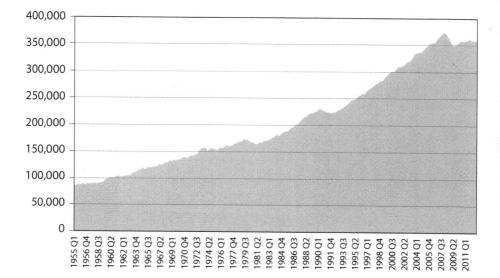

GDP

A BRIEF BUT AFFECTIONATE HISTORY

REVISED AND EXPANDED EDITION

DIANE COYLE

PRINCETON UNIVERSITY PRESS
PRINCETON AND OXFORD

press.princeton.edu

Cover typography by Jerome Corgier/Marlena Agency. Design by
Kathleen Lynch/Black Kat Design.

Library of Congress Control Number 2015936928
ISBN 978-0-691-16985-9

British Library Cataloging-in-Publication Data is available

This book has been composed in Minion Pro

Printed on acid-free paper. ∞

Printed in the United States of America

3 5 7 9 10 8 6 4

CONTENTS

NOTE ON THE PAPERBACK EDITION

Statisticians do not make the headlines very often, but they have done so, repeatedly, since this book was first published early in 2014. They increased the size of China's economy, measured by Gross Domestic Product (GDP), by a fifth, thanks to changes in the way international price comparisons are made. They nearly doubled Nigeria's GDP by updating the role rapidly growing areas of business—Nollywood movies, mobile phones—play in the statistics. Other African economies have enjoyed the same kind of GDP boost. Most titillating of all, the statisticians increased GDP in most European countries by deciding to add in estimates for prostitution and drugs, activities that are part of the illegal but nevertheless market-based economy. This move was a minor blessing for all the EU governments eager to cut the burden of government debt, which is always measured in relation to GDP; raising the denominator of this ratio is far less troublesome than reducing the numerator. But the change in methodology underlined one of the many paradoxes in this conventional measure of economic success, in that it includes prostitution but excludes unpaid work (of all kinds) in the home. What kind of statistic is GDP?

A lot of people are interested in this question. Before publication of this book, I would have been amazed if anyone had told me that there could be audiences numbering in the hundreds for a talk on the history of GDP. I think the reasons for this interest are largely those described in the final chapter here. Chapter 6 discusses the growing gap between GDP, which is a particular measure of economic activity that takes place in markets and has prices attached, and economic well-being or social welfare. Although we economists have always known in theory that GDP does not measure social welfare in any sense, we—and therefore policy makers and news commentators—have always ignored that caveat in practice. For decades now we have been taking the growth of GDP as our measure of whether we are growing more prosperous, or better off in a wider sense.

The economy has been changing in ways that increase the difference between the two concepts. GDP was a good enough measure for the assembly-line manufacturing and nation state–based economies of the post–Second World War era; now we have an economy dominated by services and intangibles, with *much* greater variety of products, and closely linked across national boundaries. It is not at all clear that GDP measures well the digital, globalized economy, with its proliferation of zero-price services and matching markets or secondhand markets. It certainly does not speak to the distribution of growth between different people or groups, which has grown far less equal since around 1980. Finally, GDP does not give us a handle on how sustainably the economy is growing, an ever more important question in the wake of both the Great Financial Crisis and increasing concerns about irreversible environmental or climate damage. So while using GDP to measure economic activity is one thing, it is becoming decreasingly useful as a proxy for either social welfare or sustainability.

The official statisticians who provide us with the wherewithal to take the temperature of the economy are therefore continuing to innovate. They are more aware than anybody of this list of challenges to the conventional use of GDP growth as the shorthand for how well we're doing. Some of their intriguing new approaches are described here too. This paperback edition brings the story of GDP up to date. I would like to thank the audiences and readers and reviewers who have provided insights and comments. However, the end of the story is not yet in sight, nor is it obvious what it will be. In ten years' time we will have a very different economy and a different way of thinking about 'the economy' and how well, or not, it is serving us.

March 2015

GDP

Introduction

"In Greece, statistics is a combat sport." Andreas Georgiou was speaking after the announcement that he would be facing criminal charges and a parliamentary inquiry. A distinguished man who had previously spent many years working at the International Monetary Fund (IMF) in Washington, DC, Georgiou could be played by George Clooney in the movie about the European economic catastrophe. In late 2010 he became the head of Elstat, Greece's new official statistical agency, parachuted into the job by the European Union (EU) and the IMF. Within weeks his emails were being hacked, and within months he was accused by recently sacked board members of the old official statistics agency of acting against Greece's national interest. In a case that has bitterly divided opinion in Greece, prosecutors subsequently charged him with the felonies of dereliction of duty, making false statements, and falsifying official data.[1] His crime? Trying to produce accurate statistics on the Greek economy after decades during which official statisticians had massaged figures at the behest of politicians. The stakes were high, as rescue funds to bail out the Greek government and prevent the economy from collapsing depended on the achievement of tough targets for reducing how much the government was spending and borrowing. The targets were expressed as a ratio of the budget deficit to GDP—Gross Domestic Product, the standard measure of the size of a country's economy. GDP is a familiar piece of jargon that doesn't actually mean much to most people. This book is the story of how this statistic came to be so important.

According to an official European Commission inquiry published just ahead of Georgiou's appointment, the Greek figures had been doctored for years. The head of the National Statistical Service of Greece (NSSG, the predecessor to Elstat) had earlier that year, in some desperation, contacted European officials in Brussels, "claiming official interference over the provision of figures." The inquiry concluded that there had been repeated misreporting of figures, that the Greek government could not keep track of its own spending anyway, and that there were grave doubts about the "accountability of the Greek institutional framework"—a bureaucratic phrase for the government's inability to control or even count its expenditure in a number of areas including defense spending.[2]

An official inquiry was in fact unnecessary. A statistician could have told the Brussels Commissioners that the Greeks were cooking the books just by looking at the reported numbers. One potential warning signal was the announcement in 2006 that Greece's GDP was 25 percent higher than previously thought: NSSG added in an estimate of the value to the economy of off-the-books activities, hidden from the tax authorities. Greece was certainly not the only country to include in official GDP figures an estimate of the size of the so-called informal economy (as we will see later), but this large boost came at a useful time for borrowing more, as the size of GDP is key to lenders' views about the borrower's capacity to repay the loan.

Apart from this change, and apart from the regular refusal by EU statisticians to approve the Greek numbers, made-up figures also have a statistical marker indicating that they have been fabricated. The pattern of GDP or other economic variables has a particular statistical fingerprint that is hard to falsify. These series of statistics are not random. Specifically, the first digit is not a 1 (or any other digit up to 9) one time in every nine, as would be the case with random statistics. Instead, the figures are far more likely to start with a 1: the first digit will be a 1 six times more often than it will be a 9, over two times more often than it will be a 3, and so on. The fingerprint pattern is known as Benford's Law. Dr. Charlie Eppes, the mathematical genius played by David Krumholtz in the crime drama *Numb3rs*, uses it to solve a series of burglaries in one 2006 episode, "The Running Man." Greek GDP statistics did not have the Benford's Law fingerprint.[3]

The European Commission report was clear—it is some of the bluntest bureaucratic language I have ever read—that Greece's Ministry of Finance was instructing the official statisticians what the deficit and GDP figures needed to be in order to keep the loans flowing. The board of NSSG before 2010 must have either known about the fabrication or not known—in which case it was hardly an effective board for a national statistical agency. As it happens, my good friend Paola Subacchi, now director of economics at the distinguished international affairs think tank Chatham House, had visited NSSG in 2002. She flew to Athens, and took a taxi to an address that turned out to be in a residential suburb. She says: "It was in a square of ordinary shops, and I had to hunt for a doorway in a 1950s apartment block that took me up some stairs to a dusty room with a handful of people. I can't remember seeing any computers. It was extraordinary, not a professional operation at all." No wonder the IMF and European Commission wanted to send in Mr. Georgiou to create a new statistical agency as a condition of lending the rescue funds to the Greek government. There might yet be nasty surprises to uncover. "I am being prosecuted for not cooking the books," he said after he was accused of betraying the national interest, a crime that in theory carries a potential life sentence. In mid-2015 he was still under legal threat.

The point of this story of nefarious statistical manipulation is to highlight the importance of GDP in everyday politics and finance. In theory, Mr. Georgiou could be imprisoned for producing a different number from his predecessors. The living standards of millions of Greek people—would they have jobs? would they need to join the lines at the soup kitchens?— depended on the figure.

GDP is the way we measure and compare how well or badly countries are doing. But this is not a question of measuring a natural phenomenon like land mass or average temperature to varying degrees of accuracy. GDP is a made-up entity. The concept dates back only to the 1940s. As the next chapter will discuss, before then different concepts were used to measure how well the economy was doing, and even they originated only just over two hundred years ago. In the unlikely event he does ever go to prison, Mr. Georgiou will have lost his liberty over an abstraction that adds up everything from nails to toothbrushes, tractors, shoes, haircuts, management consultancy, street cleaning, yoga teaching, plates, bandages, books, and all the millions of other services and products in the economy—and then adjusts them in complicated ways and for seasonal fluctuations, taking account of inflation, and standardizes them so that all countries' statistics are roughly comparable, as long as they are adjusted again for some hypothetical exchange rates. You get the point: an abstract statistic derived in extremely complicated ways, yet one that has tremendous importance.

So how has something so artificial, complicated, and abstract come to be so important for economic policies affecting the livelihood of the Greek people? Can it be right that GDP rules key political decisions affecting their fate and ours? After all, this single measure of "the economy" tends to dominate political contests, and governments' fortunes seem to rise and fall with the difference between plus 0.2 percent and minus 0.1 percent in one quarter's GDP numbers. The latter may mean recession, the former reelection. News bulletins often feature economists and politicians making strong opposing claims about how the economy is doing, by which they mean what the GDP growth rate is likely to be, and what the government should be doing as a result.

Yet the primacy of GDP as the measure of economic success has been increasingly challenged, not so much by politicians or economists as by people who see it as the primary symbol of what's gone wrong with the capitalist market economy. For example, environmentalists believe it leads to an overemphasis on growth at the expense of the planet, "happiness" advocates think it needs to be replaced with indicators of genuine well-being, and activists such as those in the Occupy movement argue that a focus on GDP has disguised inequality and social disharmony.

There are certainly several reasonable critiques of GDP and the role it has come to play in guiding economic policy. These also include questions about how complicated the statistical construction of GDP has become, and what such a complex abstraction can actually mean. But GDP is also, as this book will show too, an important measure of the freedom and human capability created by the capitalist market economy.

GDP indicates, although imperfectly, innovation and human possibility. And it is an important measure of our creativity and care for one another in an economy based more and more on services and intangibles. In 2000, the U.S. Bureau of Economic Analysis declared GDP to be "One of the Great Inventions of the 20th Century."[4] It is an understandable exaggeration.

This book explains GDP and describes its history, sets out its limitations, and defends it still as a key indicator for economic policy. It is certainly a better indicator than some of the fashionable alternatives (like "happiness") that have been proposed. I also ask whether GDP alone is still a good enough measure of economic performance—and conclude not. It is a measure designed for the twentieth-century economy of physical mass production, not for the modern economy of rapid innovation and intangible, increasingly digital, services. How well the economy is doing is always going to be an important part of everyday politics, and we're going to need a better measure of "the economy" than today's GDP.

ONE

From the Eighteenth Century to the 1930s: War and Depression

Warfare is the mother of invention. Many new technologies that end up in use in civilian life have been spurred by the demands of conflict and funded by the military. Among these inventions, ranging from the Internet to Teflon, radar to programmable electronic computers, is Gross Domestic Product. GDP is one of the many inventions of World War II.

Its name sounds as though it should be self-explanatory. *Product:* things that are produced. *Domestic:* at home. *Gross:* nothing deducted, the opposite of *net* (conversely, a cereal packet will give "net weight," meaning the contents alone, not including the packaging). GDP is just one figure in a full set of accounts for the economy, the national income accounts. We will get to the detail later. To make sense of the idea of GDP, first a brief history of the development of national statistics will help.

THE EARLY DAYS OF NATIONAL ACCOUNTING

It was an earlier war that prompted the first systematic attempts to measure the whole of the economy. In 1665, a British scientist and official, William Petty, produced estimates of the income and expenditure, population, land, and other assets of England and Wales, with the aim of assessing the country's resources to fight a conflict and finance it through taxes (it was the now little-known Second Anglo-Dutch War, which lasted from 1664 to 1667). Petty wanted to prove not only that the country could bear a higher burden of taxes but also that it was capable of taking on its powerful neighbors, Holland and France.[1] There was no need for it to win more land or increase the size of the population to ensure victory, because the available land and capital and labor could be used to better effect. This was a significant economic insight. Also significant was Petty's introduction of the tool of double-entry bookkeeping to keep records for the nation as a whole. Another early set of estimates, by Charles Davenant in 1695, had the title *An Essay upon the Ways and Means of Supplying the War*, making his aim perfectly clear. The word *statistics* has the same origin as *state*, and originally referred to the collection of figures concerning the state, specifically taxes. It proved to be a major advantage for England to have consolidated national income statistics, enabling calculations about the scope for increased output and tax revenues, when its larger and seemingly more powerful neighbor France lacked such information. Not until 1781 did the French king have similar strategically important economic and financial data, when the finance minister Jacques Necker delivered a famous *compte rendu au roi*, or report to the king, on the strength of the French economy. It enabled the king to raise new loans but did not, of course, help him avert the French Revolution in 1789.

Throughout the eighteenth century a number of successive statistical pioneers built on these first British attempts, although each was measuring slightly different things. The concept of "national income" may seem clear enough, but measuring it in practice means choosing what to include and exclude, which is surprisingly fuzzy. Unlike in our own time, there was no standardization, no commonly agreed definition; and what was measured was not at all like modern GDP. What these early national accounts had in common was the general idea that the national income depended on how much was available to spend now and how much remained for increasing the national stock of assets.

This framework evolved over the decades.[2] Later authors emphasized different aspects of the economy. Some—among them the novelist and pamphleteer Daniel Defoe—thought that the key to the nation's prosperity was increasing trade, both overseas and within the country. At another time, the debate in coffeehouses and pamphlets centered firmly on the national debt, the figures for which the government published frequently between the late seventeenth and late eighteenth centuries. Once again, financing warfare was the motivation.

Then came a substantial intellectual innovation. In *The Wealth of Nations* (published 1776), Adam Smith introduced the distinction between "productive" and "unproductive" labor. An anonymous author had written in 1746, "What I mean by National Income is, all the whole body of our People get or receive from Land, Trade, Arts, Manufactures, Labour, or any other way whatsoever; and by Annual Expence I mean, the whole that they spend or consume." Yet in Adam Smith's definition thirty years later, the "whole body of our

People" did *not* count. Only those involved in the making of physical commodities, agriculture and industry, would count toward national income. The provision of more *services* was a cost to the national economy, in his view. A servant was a cost to his employer, and did not create anything. Importantly, money spent on warfare or the interest on government debt was also being used unproductively. The nation's wealth was its stock of physical assets less the national debt. National income was what derived from the national wealth. According to Benjamin Mitra-Kahn, "*The Wealth of Nations* introduced a new idea of the economy, and through the effort of Adam Smith's students and admirers, it was adopted almost instantly."

In Smith's own words:

> There is one sort of labour which adds to the value of the subject upon which it is bestowed: There is another which has no such effect. The former, as it produces a value, may be called productive; the latter, unproductive labour. Thus the labour of a manufacturer adds, generally, to the value of the materials which he works upon, that of his own maintenance, and of his master's profit. The labour of a menial servant, on the contrary, adds to the value of nothing. . . . A man grows rich by employing a multitude of manufacturers: He grows poor, by maintaining a multitude of menial servants.[3]

The idea of a distinction between productive and unproductive activity, adopted by Adam Smith, dominated economic debate and measurement until the late nineteenth century. Karl Marx echoed it, and it remained the basis for measuring the centrally planned economies until the collapse of communism after 1989. For example, the Soviet Union's economic statistics counted material output and largely ignored service activities; yet by the late 1980s, these accounted for about two-thirds of GDP in the Western capitalist economies, so it was a large omission.

Still, this way of thinking about the national economy in terms of material production was generally adopted in the nineteenth century, until it too was overturned. Then the new generation of "neoclassical" economists (in contrast to "classical" economists such as Adam Smith) discarded the distinction between productive and unproductive activities. Alfred Marshall, as titanic a figure as Smith in the history of economic thought, said firmly: "Wealth consists of material wealth and personal or non-material wealth." Services were to be included in the definition of national income. The work done in the late nineteenth and early twentieth century to measure the economy in the wake of Marshall's decree in his 1890 book *Principles of Economics* has been described as a "first phase" of national income accounting.[4]

The Birth of Modern National Accounts

This quick dip into the early history of national income accounts and the forerunners of GDP shows that the definition of "national income" was not precise or fixed. How it was interpreted depended on the intellectual climate and on the political or military needs of the moment, and so the definition changed over time. Some economists have concluded that the pre-twentieth-century measurement of the economy was not all that serious. Angus Maddison, who spearheaded the extraordinary achievement of constructing GDP statistics for the world dating back to AD1000, wrote, "Economic growth was much slower before the 19th century and therefore seemed irrelevant or uninteresting."[5] He added, a bit sniffily: "Although there was a proliferation of national income estimates, there was little improvement in their quality or comparability. They provided little help for serious analysis of economic growth, and there were significant differences in their coverage and methodology." The early work was certainly not consistent over the years, nor consistent with our modern definitions. But the opposite interpretation seems likely: from the nineteenth century, people were starting to reconsider how to measure the economy precisely because it was starting to grow, thanks to the Industrial Revolution and the dawn of capitalism.

The definitions we use now date back to two seismic events in modern history, the Great Depression of the 1930s and World War II (1939–1945).[6]

Following the publication of Alfred Marshall's *Principles of Economics*, a number of researchers had already set about new efforts to improve the collection of statistics and the measurement of national income. In the United Kingdom, the most successful was due to Colin Clark, who throughout the 1920s and 1930s calculated national income and expenditure, for the first time on a quarterly rather than an annual basis, and with a new degree of care and thoroughness. For example, he provided detailed splits of production and expenditure into different categories and published thorough accounts of the government's finances, too. He discussed how to adjust the figures for inflation, and also the distribution of income among different categories of people. Clark was appointed in 1930 to provide statistics to the newly created National Economic Advisory Council, the first body ever created by the British government to provide formal economic advice. The experience of the Depression created this demand for statistics that might help the government figure out how to bring to an end the unprecedented economic slump.

Across the Atlantic, in the United States, Simon Kuznets had a similar motivation. The government of Franklin Delano Roosevelt wanted a clearer picture of the state of an economy trapped in a seemingly endless depression. The National Bureau of Economic Research was requested to provide estimates of national income. Kuznets, who later won the Nobel Memorial Prize in Economic Science for this work, took on the task of developing Clark's methods and applying them to the U.S. economy. He was a meticulous collector and assembler of data, paying careful attention to the circumstances in which different statistics were gathered, and what their flaws might therefore be.[7] His first report, submitted to Congress in January 1934, showed that America's national income had been halved between 1929 and 1932. Even in those depressed times the report was a bestseller, at twenty cents a copy, and the first print run of forty-five hundred copies quickly sold out.[8] President Roosevelt cited the figures in announcing the new Recovery Program and used updated figures (running up to 1937) to send a supplemental budget to Congress in 1938. As one survey of the history of national accounting points out, having national income estimates for the whole economy made a huge difference to the scope for policy. President Herbert Hoover had made do with the incomplete picture painted by industrial statistics such as share price indexes and freight car loadings. This information was less compelling, as a call to action, than an authoritative figure showing the halving of the whole of national economic output in the space of just a few years.

Kuznets, however, specifically saw his task as working out how to measure national economic *welfare* rather than just *output*. He wrote:

It would be of great value to have national income estimates that would remove from the total the elements which, from the standpoint of a more enlightened social philosophy than that of an acquisitive society represent dis-service rather than service. Such estimates would subtract from the present national income totals all expenses on armament, most of the outlays on advertising, a great many of the expenses involved in financial and speculative activities, and what is perhaps most important, the outlays that have been made necessary in order to overcome difficulties that are, properly speaking, costs implicit in our economic civilization. All the gigantic outlays in our urban civilization, subways, expensive housing, etc., which in our usual estimates we include at the value of the net product they yield on the market, do not really represent net services to the individuals comprising the nation but are, from their viewpoint, an evil necessary in order to be able to make a living.[9]

These observations prefigure some of the criticisms made of GDP in our own time: GDP definitely does not attempt to measure welfare or well-being (a subject picked up again in chapters 5 and 6).

With this aim, in fact, Kuznets was out of tune with his times. Welfare was a peacetime luxury. This passage was written in 1937, when his first set of accounts was presented to Congress. Before long, the president would want a way of measuring the economy that did indicate its total capacity to produce but did *not* show additional government expenditure on armaments as reducing the nation's output. The trouble with the prewar definitions of national income was precisely that as constructed they would show the economy shrinking if private output available for consumption declined, even if the government spending required for the war effort was expanding output elsewhere in the economy. The Office of Price Administration and Civilian Supply, established in 1941, found that its recommendation to increase government expenditure in the subsequent year was rejected on this basis. Changing the definition of national income to the concept of GDP, rather than something more like Kuznets's original proposal, overcame this hurdle.

There was a heated debate between Kuznets and other economists, especially Milton Gilbert of the Commerce Department, about the right approach. The discussions were highly technical but the underlying issue was profound: what was the meaning of economic growth and why were statisticians measuring it? Gilbert and his colleagues were clear that the aim was to have a measurement that was useful to the government in running its fiscal policy. As one of the pioneers of GDP put it, rather blandly: "It will be convenient if the incomings and outgoings of public authorities in the provision and organization of common services such as defence, justice, education and public health are thought of as consolidated in the consumption box, being in fact nothing more than agency activities for the body of consumers as a whole."[10] An official U.S. history of the national income accounts describes it this way:

> Before GNP [Gross National Product] was made available, projected defense expenditures were sometimes erroneously subtracted from projected national income, producing a residual that was interpreted as the amount of production left for non-war goods and services.... The assessment was overly grim because national income fell short of the total market value of goods and services produced, of which defense spending was a component....
>
> By including all government purchases as part of national products, the GNP statistics established the role of national government in the economy as that of an ultimate consumer, that is as a purchase of goods and services for final use.[11]

The first American GNP statistics were published in 1942, distinguishing between the types of expenditure, including by government, and permitted economists to see the economy's potential for war production. "The inclusion of business taxes and depreciation [in GNP measured at market prices] resulted in a production measure that was more appropriate for analysis of the war program's burden on the economy."[12] Kuznets was highly skeptical: "He argued that Commerce's method tautologically ensured that fiscal spending would increase measured economic growth regardless of whether it actually benefited individuals' economic welfare."[13] In the policy tussle in Washington, Kuznets lost and wartime realpolitik won.

This decision was a turning point in the measurement of national income, and it meant that GNP (or later GDP) would be a concept strikingly different from the way the economy had been thought about from the dawn of modern industrial growth in the early eighteenth century until the early twentieth century. For two centuries, "the economy" was the private sector. Government played a small role in economic life, and featured mainly because it looked to raise taxes to pay for wars. Its role expanded steadily over the centuries, however. In Victorian times this began to extend to the provision of other services, those we take for granted now such as roads and water as well as the historic government roles of defense and justice. By the time the wartime economists developed the modern concept of GDP, government was already a far greater presence than it had been. Subtracting defense spending from the older conception of national income would have wrongly given the impression that the war effort was going to involve a huge sacrifice in private consumer spending. There is, of course, a world of difference between a monarch extracting tax revenues to wage war and a democratic government pooling citizens' incomes to provide services and social security. One aspect of this democratic transition was the switch to conceiving of government as adding to national income rather than subtracting from it. However, the importance of wartime necessity in shaping the definition should not be underestimated. The pattern of growth before and after 1945 would have looked very different if government spending had been disregarded as before in the definition of total economic activity.

The United Kingdom, already since 1939 at war with Germany and its allies, had earlier reached the same conclusion as the U.S. officials. Colin Clark's approach was overtaken and extended when the brilliant and influential John Maynard Keynes published in 1940 the pamphlet *How to Pay for the War*. He fulminated in this about the inadequacy of the statistics available to him for calculating what the U.K. economy could produce with the available resources, what would be required for mobilization and conflict, what would be left over for people to consume—and how much their living standards might need to fall. Planning for the war effort in particular needed much better statistics on how much was produced by individual industries, using what materials. Keynes wrote, "Every government since the last war has been unscientific and obscurantist, and has regarded the collection of essential facts as a waste of money."[14]

Other countries were separately developing the concept and measurement of GDP during the 1930s. Holland was another pioneer, as were Germany and the Soviet Union. But the motivating force of being at war should not be underestimated. Wesley C. Mitchell, the director of the National Bureau of Economic Research, said: "Only those who had a personal share in the economic mobilization for war could realize in how many ways and how much estimates of national income covering 20 years and classified in several ways facilitated the World War II effort."[15]

A senior British Treasury official, Austin Robinson, was so impressed by Keynes's argument in *How to Pay for the War* that he commissioned two young economists, Richard Stone and James Meade, to develop what became the first modern set of national accounts and GDP. These were published with the U.K. government's budget of 1941. Keynes did not have an official post, but was given an office in the Treasury and oversaw the work and the subsequent establishment of the Central Statistical Office, a new official statistical agency. In 1984, Stone was awarded the Nobel Memorial Prize in Economic Science for his contribution to developing GDP and the national accounts (Meade had won the award earlier for his work on trade theory). Stone went on to be particularly influential in the postwar coordination and standardization of the definitions and measurements of GDP. This began as a discussion between the British and American experts. In May 1946, a Committee of Statistical Experts met at Hunter College in New York to draw up recommendations for collecting national statistics on behalf of the United Nations.

The planning required during the conflict continued to be needed in the period of rebuilding after the end of World War II. George Marshall, the then U.S. secretary of state, used a speech at Harvard University on 5 June 1947 to announce U.S. support for postwar reconstruction. He said:

> Aside from the demoralizing effect on the world at large and the possibilities of disturbances arising as a result of the desperation of the people concerned, the consequences to the economy of the United States should be apparent to all. It is logical that the United States should do whatever it is able to do to assist in the return of normal economic health in the world, without which there can be no political stability and no assured peace. Our policy is directed not against any country or doctrine but against hunger, poverty, desperation and chaos. Its purpose should be

the revival of a working economy in the world so as to permit the emergence of political and social conditions in which free institutions can exist.[16]

The administration of President Harry Truman lived up to this vision and provided total aid worth an estimated $148 billion (in 2004 dollars) from 1946 to 1952.[17] The devastated countries of Europe depended heavily on Marshall Aid to enable them to survive and rebuild. Throughout that period everything was in short supply and tracking the use of resources was essential. Before long, the United Nations took on the responsibility for setting international standards of measurement in what is now known as the System of National Accounts (SNA).

Once available, these statistics on the whole economy found another use. Keynes had wanted to have the figures available for the purpose of wartime planning. But he had also published just before the war his massively influential book *The General Theory of Employment, Interest and Money*. At the heart of this classic economic text lies a theory about the relationship between different economic variables, including, in addition to national income, personal consumption, investment and employment, interest rates, and the level of government spending. The theory set out links between the tools the government had available and the size of the economy. It became the basis for a more interventionist approach to government economic policy from the 1940s onward, using both fiscal policy (the level of tax and spending) and monetary policy (the level of interest rates and availability of credit) to target a higher and less volatile rate of growth for the economy. The use of these tools was developed more fully by other economists after Keynes's early death in April 1946. Postwar policymakers still bore the scars of the Great Depression and pounced on the economic theories of Keynes and his successors as a means of averting a repetition of that crisis. Crucially, the development of GDP, and specifically its inclusion of government expenditure, winning out over Kuznets's welfare-based approach made Keynesian macroeconomic theory the fundamental basis of how governments ran their economies in the postwar era. The conceptual measurement change enabled a significant change in the part governments were to play in the economy. GDP statistics and Keynesian macroeconomic policy were mutually reinforcing. The story of GDP since 1940 is also the story of macroeconomics. The availability of national accounts statistics made demand management seem not only feasible but also scientific.

This sense of control was enhanced by the parallel development of methods for using national accounts statistics to estimate econometric "models" of the economy. The pioneer here was a Dutch economist (and the first winner of the Nobel Memorial Prize in Economic Science), Jan Tinbergen, his country having been almost as rapid in adopting GDP as the United Kingdom and the United States. A macroeconomic model is a series of equations representing certain relationships, for example between interest rates and investment, or consumer spending and incomes. Econometric techniques are the statistical methods used to estimate these relationships on the basis of past statistics—for example, that consumers will spend 40 percent of an increase in personal income. The models estimated on *past* averages can then be used to predict what might happen in the future, especially if the government changes some of its policies, say, increasing personal taxes. For example, a one-million-dollar increase in government spending (or cut in taxes) will put more disposable income in the pockets of taxpayers, who will spend some of the extra on goods and services. The people benefiting from that additional business will have higher incomes themselves, and spend more in turn. A key question is how big the final increase in GDP will turn out to be. That depends on other factors: how much extra actually gets spent rather than saved; how much interest rates rise because there's more demand for borrowing; how much is spent on imports rather than goods and services produced at home; how much inflation rises because the additional demand exceeds what is supplied in the short term. As economists would put it, the additional government spending can either "crowd in" or "crowd out" private spending. In the former case, the fiscal "multiplier" exceeds one, and in the latter case is less than one—some estimates have it actually being negative. The multiplier is a measure of how much GDP changes compared to the change in government spending (or tax revenues).

Although Keynes himself was highly skeptical about econometric models, they became a key tool in the more interventionist approach to government economic policy that prevailed from the late 1940s until the economic crisis of the late 1970s. In fact, the number of models proliferated, and a new forecasting industry was created by pioneers such as Otto Eckstein, the founder of Data Resources, Incorporated (DRI).[18] We are now awash with macroeconomic models and forecasts, published by official agencies and central banks, by investment banks, by think tanks and researchers, as well as by commercial forecasters such as DRI's successors. Indeed, the idea of the economy as a machine, regulated by appropriate policy levers, took firm hold. Such firm hold that the engineer-turned-economist Bill Phillips built an actual machine showing the flow of income in the economy and the routes through which government policy could increase that flow (see figure 1). A few of the machines remain in universities, as curiosities—but the "engineering" mindset still has a firm grip on economic policy.

Figure 1. Phillips Machine, courtesy of the Library of the London School
of Economics and Political Science, IMAGELIBRARY/6

For macroeconometric models are still in widespread use, even though the earlier illusion of precise control ought to have been shattered by events over the course of the decades since the 1940s. Governments after all still need to try to forecast what the effect of their interventions and policy changes might be. They are now far more complicated and subtle than earlier generations of macroeconomic models (partly because the economy has become more complicated), and importantly include the influence of expectations about the future on current links between economic variables. Nonetheless, the financial and economic crisis since 2008—not predicted by mainstream economic forecasters—has led to an active debate about whether the approach of aggregating individual behavior and assuming stable links between the aggregate measures (that is, the statistics defined in the national accounts) is a valid exercise. Debate rages in particular about the multiplier, because the issue of whether extra government spending or tax cuts (a "fiscal stimulus") will boost GDP growth turns on its size. If it is greater than one, a stimulus of extra government spending will help growth, while austerity measures will hurt it. Its actual size is hotly contested among macroeconomists, especially in the context of the present political debate about how much "fiscal stimulus" the government should be applying to get the economy growing faster. There is an unsurprising alignment in the "multiplier wars" between macroeconomists' answer to the technical question about the size of the multiplier and their political sympathies. In early 2013, after some years of austerity measures cutting government spending in European countries and Japan, the IMF's chief economist concluded that, contrary to the Fund's earlier official view, the multipliers on fiscal policy in the early years of the crisis were substantially above one, or in other words that austerity measures had done more harm than good to short-term GDP growth.[19] The paper also makes it clear, however, that multipliers vary among countries and over time (although estimates are typically greater than one), so the mechanical approach to macroeconomic modeling that developed alongside the creation of today's GDP and national accounts figures remains in question.

THE NATURE OF GDP

It will be clear by now that the ambition of measuring national income has a long history, with correspondingly many changes in how people have thought about it. As Richard Stone put it, national income is not a "primary fact" but an "empirical construct": "To ascertain income it is necessary to set up a theory from which income is derived as a concept by postulation and then associate this concept with a certain set of primary facts."[20]

There is no such entity as GDP out there in the real world waiting to be measured by economists. It is an abstract idea, and one that after a half century of international discussion and standard-setting has become extremely complicated. The manuals for statisticians run to hundreds of pages, and it takes a substantial investment of time and effort to understand the national accounts in any detail. Now, though, it's time to set out the basics.

What Is It? Definitions

It is surprisingly hard to write down definitions of GDP that do not assume some prior knowledge. So this section will seem complicated for GDP novices, and yet will be considered laughably oversimplified by national accounts experts.

Understanding GDP is a bit like a video game with increasing levels of difficulty.

The system for measuring GDP and its components has steadily become more and more complicated, too. This is because of the increasing sophistication of the statistical methods used, and because of the increasing complexity of the economy itself. For example, a growing proportion of the economy consists of services, whose output is inherently *uncertainty* harder to measure than the output of, say, tractors or cotton fabric. The first UN guide to the SNA, which all countries are supposed to follow, was published in 1953 and had fewer than fifty pages. The 2008 SNA document has 722 pages. A widely used commentary on the SNA has four hundred pages.[21] The community of national statisticians with a command of all this detail is small. In other words, very few people indeed truly understand how the regularly published GDP figures are constructed—this excludes many of the economists who comment on GDP. So, take a deep breath before embarking on the next few pages.

To start with the basics, GDP can be measured in three ways, in principle equivalent to one another. You can add up all the *output* of the economy, all the *expenditure* in the economy, or all the *incomes*. Table 1 shows these three and their components, including their shares in the U.S. economy in 2005.

The rest of this section concerns GDP, but before continuing, it should be noted that another way of defining an economy's total output is Gross *National* Product. GDP counts all the economic output generated within the nation's boundary. GNP counts all the economic output generated by national entities, some of it occurring overseas. In other words, the main difference between the two is that GNP also includes output or income from overseas. For a few small countries (such as Ireland and Luxembourg), the difference is large.

Table 1: Three Ways to Measure GDP

I. Value-added (or production) approach	2005 share (percent)
Gross output (gross sales less change in inventories)	183.5
Less: Intermediate inputs	83.5
Equals: **Value added for each industry**	**100.0**

II. Income (by type) approach	
Sum of: Compensation	56.6
Rental income	0.3
Profits and proprietors' income	17.6
Taxes on production and imports	7.4
Less: Subsidies	0.5
Interest, miscellaneous payments	5.5
Depreciation	12.9
Equals: **Total domestic incomes earned**	**100.0**

III. Final demand (or expenditures) approach	
Sum of: Consumption of final goods and services by households	70.0
Investment in plant, equipment, and software	16.7
Government expenditures on goods and services	19.0
Net exports of goods and services (exports – imports)	−5.7
Equals: **Final sales of domestic product to purchasers**	**100.0**

Source: J. Steven Landefeld, Eugene P. Seskin, and Barbara M. Fraumeni, "Taking the Pulse of the Economy: Measuring GDP," *Journal of Economic Perspectives* 22, no. 2 (2008): 193–216.

For most it is not. GDP has largely displaced GNP since the start of the modern era of globalization, although arguably economists should pay more attention to divergences between the two. GDP is also a "gross" measure in that it does not make any adjustment for the depreciation of assets (in other words, the wear and tear that reduces their value over time)—deducting this would give net domestic product. In

The Circular Flow

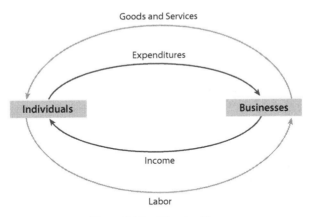

Figure 2. The Circular Flow

some ways this is a more interesting measure (the reasons are covered in chapter 6), but it is rarely referred to in everyday discussions about the economy.

Back to GDP.

Sometimes it is described as a mystical-sounding "circular flow," as illustrated in figure 2 (and built into the pipes and tubes of the Phillips Machine).

What this means is that the national accounts, like any accounts, add up on each side of the books. One consumer's spending is a business's sales revenue—when added up for the whole economy, these corresponding flows of money have to balance.

The approach to measuring GDP most familiar from the newspapers and TV is the expenditures approach. Commentators talk about consumers opening their wallets or businesses reining back investment. The equation

$$GDP = C + I + G + (X - M)$$

—consumer spending plus investment spending plus government spending plus exports less imports (the trade surplus or deficit)—will be known to anyone who has taken an introductory economics course.

So the idea seems simple. GDP is the sum of all that is spent in the national economy. Expenditures are divided into several categories. Following Keynes, these are C, consumption (by private individuals or households); I, investment (by companies); G, government expenditure (on goods and services—but not transfer payments such as welfare or pensions); and X – M, exports less imports.[22] Each can be further divided into subcategories, such as spending on food, or investment in buildings, or government expenditure on education.

The practical reality is very complicated, a matter of finicky attention to detail. For example, what does measuring C mean in practice? To quote from one explanatory article, "The commodity flow method starts with total sales (or shipments) by producers of final goods and services. Then using this estimate of final sales, the bureau adds (a) transportation costs (b) wholesale and retail trade margins (c) sales taxes and (d) imports. It then deducts (e) changes in inventories (f) exports (g) sales to business (because these are intermediate goods) and (h) sales to government. The method produces consistent estimates of the value of final sales to consumers."[23] And so on.

Then there are fuzzy boundaries—for example, should a consumer's purchase of a car she will use for ten years be counted as "consumption" when a company's purchase of software it will use for only two years is classed as "investment"? The change in the amount of inventory or stock held by businesses will have to be included, even though it is likely to change in response to events rather than deliberate business choice. Some elements of expenditure are estimates of the value of services not purchased directly: the value of living in an owner-occupied house is one example.

The approach of adding up everything produced in the economy (the value-added approach) is even simpler to set out, as in table 1, but again in practice requires a lot of careful calculation of the separate elements. The total adds up everything that is produced in the economy, all the goods and services. Almost every business will use in its production the output of other businesses, however. So to avoid double counting, these purchases of "intermediate" goods have to be excluded, netted off from final sales.[24] At first this was a tricky matter of patching together different sources of data. But in the 1950s, Wassily Leontief (another Nobel Memorial Prize–winning economist) came up with the idea of input-output tables that tracked the sale and purchases of intermediate goods through the economy to calculate the "value added" in production. From the mid-1960s this method has been used to publish the production side of the national accounts. (In the USSR, Gosplan, the central planning agency, adopted the same approach, publishing the first Soviet input-output tables in 1959.)

Another important practicality is to adjust for normal seasonal fluctuations. It is not helpful to know that consumers spent more in the October–December quarter than in the July–September quarter, as the holidays alone will mean higher spending every year. We want to know whether this year's increase was unusually large or small. So there are statistical techniques for "seasonal adjustment" to give figures that smooth out the normal ups and downs over the year. The figures analyzed by economists and pronounced on by the media are all these seasonally adjusted ones. The statistical bureau takes the initial figures and adjusts them for "normal" seasonal patterns. Abnormal changes in the pattern, such as an unusually hot summer, or a holiday falling on a Thursday so everyone takes a long weekend, can play havoc with the adjustment process.

All of the transactions included in GDP are measured at the price paid for them in the market—when these are available. Government spending, for example, is by definition not in a marketplace, so it has to be valued either by how much the government pays in salaries to the people working in the service, or how much a similar service would cost if purchased privately. An alternative is to measure GDP at factor cost, which adjusts the market price paid by deducting VAT or sales tax and adding in any government subsidy that reduced the price. The "factor cost adjustment" is the gap between the two GDP totals.

As noted a few pages back, the "gross" part of GDP indicates that expenditure is not adjusted for spending on wear-and-tear or obsolescence. This affects some household purchases but more so business investment in assets that need maintenance and repair or need replacing after time. An estimate of depreciation can be deducted from GDP to give net domestic product.

The "accounting" in the national accounts means that the sum of all spending in the economy must, by definition, add up to the sum of all incomes in the economy. These are classed by category—income from employment, from self-employment, from dividends and interest, business profits, income from overseas, and so on. In reality, as expenditures and incomes are collected from completely different sources of data, and a wide range of them too, they will never quite match. The statistical mismatch can be large from time to time. The U.S. and U.K. official statistics publish the discrepancy.

So far, this has been about "nominal" measures, that is, dollar or pound sterling amounts. For the purposes of economic policy, the split between inflation and "real" growth is needed. Achieving higher (nominal) GDP growth through inflation alone would be a bad sign about economic management; that was what happened in the mid-1970s when in many countries governments responded badly to big hikes in the price of oil and got the mix of slow or negative real GDP growth and high inflation labeled "stagflation." Nominal GDP continued to grow even though living standards were falling and unemployment was rising. So, to calculate real GDP statisticians have to collect data on prices and combine that into a general price index, the GDP deflator.

There are many different ways of creating a price index and calculating inflation. It will be no surprise to learn that inflation-adjustment is very complicated, perhaps one of the most challenging of all the methodological statistical issues. The calculation involves prices and quantities of each component element in the base year and the later year, often weighted depending on the different proportions of each item sold in either the base year or later year. The prices of all the goods and services in the economy are combined according to how much of each is sold. The "weight" given to each item therefore reflects how significant it is in that year's economic activity. The resulting number is "rebased" to be equal to 100 in a chosen year. The next year's price index is calculated applying the same weights to the increase in each price between one year and the next. The result will be a number like 102.5 or 104.3 (if it is less than 100, the price level has declined). This is used to divide into the later year's money GDP level, giving a "real" GDP level in terms of the base year's dollars or pounds. The importance of this adjustment will crop up again later.

I hope this sounds moderately straightforward. Unfortunately, there are dozens of different ways of calculating the formula, all with different results.[25] So, although we definitely want to make this adjustment for inflation to measure real economic growth, the choice of technique can lead to strikingly different "real" conclusions.

Is Africa Poor?

You might think that this is a straightforward question to answer; after all, the concepts "Africa" and "poverty" are closely linked in the minds of Westerners. It is harder than it seems, however, and this shows why the horrible technicalities involved in constructing GDP statistics, described briefly in the previous section, matter a lot. Specifically, take the question of whether or not Ghana is a poor country. Aid organizations use a threshold in terms of real GDP per capita set by the World Bank to designate whether a country is "low-income" or "middle-income," and this in turn determines the kind of assistance it gets in aid and cheap loans. Until November 2010, Ghana was considered "low-income," that is, a poor country. But between 5 and 6 November 2010, its GDP increased by *60 percent* overnight, turning it officially into a "low-middle-income" country. The reality had not changed, but the GDP statistics had, because the country's statistical agency had updated the weights used in calculating the price index, and consequently real GDP, for the first time since 1993. Other African economies have been following suit. Nigeria, already one of Africa's largest economies, added 89 percent to its GDP in one swoop in 2014, taking it well past South Africa in size, just by taking account of changes including the growth of booming industries like mobile telecommunications and Nollywood movies.[26] Kenya, another country with a rapidly growing mobile technology sector, added 25 per cent to its level of GDP through statistical revisions. Other African countries will be following suit. So Africa as a whole probably is not as poor as we've long thought, although nothing real in any of these economies has changed with the revisions, and they are certainly nowhere near as rich as the United Kingdom or the United States.

The trouble with using old weights is that the structure of the economy changes quite dramatically over time. In many African, Asian, and Latin American economies, the GDP calculations take no account of phenomena such as globalization, or the mobile phone revolution in the developing world. The African governments have been keen to update their statistics recently, to tell a different story about their countries, but China's has not. Its data revisions in 2014 added 3.4 per cent to the level of GDP but China did not—for now—adopt the international 'System of National Accounts,' which would have led to a much larger upward revision, because its government prefers China not to be seen as a rich country.

Donors to the poor countries have been funding efforts to improve the way real GDP is calculated—there is an initiative known as PARIS21 (Partnership in Statistics for Development in the 21st Century)—but the planned improvements stretch out to 2020 and beyond.[27] There are fundamental weaknesses with the collection of basic statistics such as what businesses there are, what they are selling, or what goods and services households spend their incomes on. The surveys needed to collect this information are carried out only infrequently. In fact, a recent study found that in the data set frequently used by economists to make international comparisons, twenty-four out of forty-five countries had no price survey data at all.[28] Some countries are using weights that have not been changed since 1968, and only ten sub-Saharan

African countries use weights less than a decade old.[29] In each case where old weights have been used for years, there will be large upward revisions in estimated real GDP when the weights are updated. This could profoundly change our impression of the character and weakness or strength of these economies; one estimate suggests that for twenty years sub-Saharan African economies have been growing three times faster than suggested by the "official" data (although, to emphasize the point, there has been no change in the extent of poverty or people's living standards because of the statistical changes).[30]

For this reason, the developed economies' national accounts for the most part now use a "chain-weighted" price index in the calculation of real GDP, meaning that the weights used to combine the separate prices into one index change steadily year by year. Otherwise, as just described, the weights in any given base year would diverge further and further from the actual pattern of the economy. The main catch with this method is that the "real terms" components of GDP no longer add up to the total: the equation $C + I + G + (X - M) = GDP$ no longer holds for the chain-weight inflation-adjusted figures. (This is because there is always a residual left over, often small but not always, when some prices and therefore weights have changed a lot.)

Chain-weighting also tells a different big-picture story about the economy, just as rebasing does. For example, historic GDP statistics such as those developed by Angus Maddison for the Organization for Economic Cooperation and Development (OECD) have not been recalculated using chain weights. To do so would change the accepted picture of international growth patterns. Maddison noted, "Acceptance of the new measure for this period [pre-1950] would involve a major reinterpretation of American history." It would show

U.S. productivity lower than the United Kingdom's in 1914, for example, and much lower U.S. growth and level of GDP than the United Kingdom's by 1929.[31] This is certainly not the received wisdom among economic historians, which matters because their explanations of what drives growth—with great relevance for policies now—could turn out to be based on an inaccurate understanding of what the economy was "really" doing in the nineteenth and twentieth centuries. Just as with developing countries now, changing the method of calculating a price index presents a different pattern of growth. The seemingly technical issue of how best to calculate a price index has some profound implications, ones which economists routinely ignore. In short, the choice of techniques completely alters even the broad outlines of the big picture on economic growth.

Silicon Valley Statistical Headaches

Silicon Valley has caused official statisticians no end of headaches. The price you had to pay for a laptop may have declined somewhat, but the price you had to pay for a unit of processing power absolutely plummeted. Similarly with other products and services such as cameras or mobile telephones or Internet connectivity. This is another particularly thorny problem related to inflation in the prices of certain types of item. Sometimes an increase in the price of an item reflects an improvement in *quality*, and failing to take account of this would lead to an underestimate of real GDP. For many years, this issue was ignored. But the amazingly rapid improvement in computers and consumer electronics from the mid-1990s made it too big to sweep under the carpet. In the United States this question was investigated by the Boskin Commission. Its 1996 report concluded that failure to take account of productivity improvements had led to an overstatement of inflation (and corresponding understatement of real growth) of 1.3 percentage points a year before 1996, about half of this due to new products and quality improvements.[32] Subsequently, official statisticians in most countries have gradually switched to using a method called "hedonic price" measurement to calculate a price index for goods and services of this kind. This involves taking the actual prices paid and calculating how those relate to various quality characteristics of the items in question. It is yet another complexity in the production of GDP statistics. The final chapter will pick up on this issue again.

Britain's Noncrisis of 1976

The 1970s, as discussed in chapter 3, were a terrible decade for the economy (as well as for fashion and haircuts). Growth was low; inflation was high. Britain did particularly badly and had a ballooning trade deficit—so large, relative to GDP, that it was not clear the country would have enough foreign currency to pay for its imports. The financial markets lost confidence and the value of the pound plunged. The chancellor of the exchequer Denis Healey was on his way to the airport for a trip to Washington when, dramatically, he had to turn back and give a press conference announcing that the United Kingdom was asking the IMF for an emergency loan. Its condition was that the government's fiscal deficit had to be slashed as a proportion of GDP. The Labour government introduced savage public spending cuts. Three years later, Margaret Thatcher swept to power in a Conservative government. Later—some time later—both the borrowing and the GDP figures were revised to an extent suggesting that the "crisis" hadn't actually been all that bad. Reflecting on the crisis in later years, Healey said, "If we had had the right figures, we would never have needed to go for the loan."[33] Who knows whether Mrs. Thatcher would have won the same kind of election victory if her predecessors in power had not had to bring in the IMF?

There is always pressure on the statisticians to produce timely data, so early estimates of the previous quarter's GDP will almost always be revised subsequently as more of the component sources of data become available. These revisions can be significant, which makes life frustrating for policy-makers trying to figure out what, if anything, they need to do to respond to the business cycle. Although the notion of "fine-tuning" the economy by adjusting tax and spending or interest rates has been pretty much discredited among economists, thanks to the terrible experience of this approach going wrong in the 1970s, there is still immense pressure on politicians and central bankers to try to boost the growth of GDP during a recession. The years of lackluster growth seen since the start of the financial crisis in 2008 are just such a period; a 2014 upward revision of 0.1 percentage point to past data removed the 'double dip' recession everybody thought had occurred post-crisis. Even though a quarterly decline of, say, 0.1 or 0.2 percent in GDP could easily be revised to zero or an increase as the weeks go by and new estimates are published, knowing this seems to do nothing to reduce the expectation that the government should take action.

This isn't the end of the list of practical but consequential difficulties in constructing GDP figures. There is the question of actually *collecting* all the statistics. Many, many separate sources of data are used, from large-scale surveys of the economy such as the five-yearly economic census by the U.S.

Bureau of Economic Analysis, to monthly figures for the production of specific goods collected by trade bodies or in replies to official questionnaires sent to a sample of businesses, to prices sampled by the statistical bureaus, to tax returns, and many more. There are, once again, numerous practical issues. One is the constant difficulty of collecting data measuring the services sector of the economy, now the major part of GDP. The standard surveys used to collect information from businesses do not cover much of the service sector. Another example is the difficulty of keeping track of changing purchasing habits. Consumers have moved progressively from purchasing in local stores to shopping in large stores, including discount "big-box" stores—where businesses may also buy some of their supplies. Now spending is shifting online. A third example is estimating the value of income received in the form of deferred stock options, once a small part of total remuneration but now quite significant. Anyway, there are errors in collecting the figures; I met one man who told me it used to be his job to fill out the forms from the statistics office, but he was too busy so he simply added a bit to the previous year's numbers.

The actual number for GDP is therefore the product of a vast patchwork of statistics and a complicated set of processes carried out on the raw data to fit them to the conceptual framework.

The "Production Boundary"

As if all of this were not enough, there are some important conceptual questions about the GDP definition, some of which will be followed up in later chapters. The definitions have evolved over the years, and there are areas of active debate among national statistics experts.

Much of GDP is private-sector output or expenditure measured at the prices charged in the market, as mentioned earlier. But large portions of output are not marketed—everything done by the government, for one thing. This has to be valued in a variety of other ways, such as the wages paid to government employees. Some of the government spending ought to be deducted, as it consists of intermediate goods: just as the purchases of nails by a furniture manufacturer would be removed to avoid double counting, so should the part of government spending such as waste removal or fire-fighting services that are intermediate inputs to final output. But that isn't done, mainly because the allocation between final and intermediate public services is impossible in practice.

Other nonmarketed items include the value homeowners get from their own homes despite not having to pay rent; the statisticians "impute" a value to this by looking at rents in the market. But some nonmarketed parts of output, such as unpaid work in the home, are not counted on the grounds that this is also too hard to measure. This results in the paradox (to which we will return in chapter 5) that a widower who marries his housekeeper and stops paying her a wage reduces GDP.

Decisions like these concern what is known as the "production boundary": what counts as economic output? Government expenditure and household services (such as cleaning and home-grown vegetables) are just two obvious fuzzy areas. The OECD's *Handbook* comments: "There is general consensus favouring the inclusion in GDP of the services provided by general government. Although these services are not sold, they are included as output (value added) in the national accounts and called non-market services produced by general government. This value added is very substantial, since it represents roughly 15% to 20% of GDP, depending on the OECD country concerned."[34] As we will see, however, this "general consensus" is relatively recent.

There is an equally general consensus that household services should not be included—although including their value (as discussed in chapter 6) might add 50 percent or more to estimates of GDP, much more than the scale of the government contribution.

There is a wider issue about production on "own-account," as it's described. Just as households decide, in producing meals, whether to grow vegetables or buy them, businesses have to decide whether to buy supplies, such as components or payroll services, or produce them for themselves. If they choose production for themselves, these components and services will not be measured in GDP; they will be used up during the process of production. If they outsource, however, these components and services will count toward the output measured in GDP. For this reason, national statisticians focus on the idea of value added, a measure independent of the way firms organize themselves. It is the value a firm adds to the intermediate goods and services it uses. Value added is equal to output (sales plus change in inventories) less purchases.

Besides, it isn't always clear when to count purchases as intermediate goods or, by contrast, investment spending. Before 2008, national accounts treated businesses' spending on R&D in the same way as spending on raw materials or cleaners; that is, as an intermediate good that would not count toward final output. This is starting to change; henceforth, R&D is supposed to be counted as investment. This change of category has already been applied in theory (since 1993) to spending on software, leading to upward revisions of 1–4 percent in the level of GDP, depending on the country, but in practice it is hard to implement because many firms do not record their spending on software as an investment.

There is a final area of the economy that poses great difficulty, and that is financial services—chapter 5 will return to this in more depth. The financial crisis has clearly raised some questions about whether the statistical treatment of financial services is right: are they making the contribution to the economy we were all assuming before 2008?

Finally, and above all, it is important to recognize that GDP is **not** a measure of welfare. It—notoriously—counts the services of lawyers and other "bads" as a positive. So too the rebuilding of bridges and homes after a storm like Katrina or Sandy, or floods. GDP measures output; it does not measure well-being. Much more on this, too, as this brief history unfolds.

TWO

1945 to 1975: The Golden Age

Let's pick up the story of GDP in the aftermath of World War II. Warfare is devastating in so many ways. The total conflict that ended in 1945 had an enormous cost in human lives and physical assets. This was particularly true in the case of the defeated countries, whose cities, factories, bridges, roads, and homes had been destroyed in the final part of the conflict. Germany, Japan, Spain, and Italy all ended the war with their countries and economies in ruins. The United Kingdom and France, although victorious, fared little better and owed large debts to the United States. After World War I, the victors had decided that defeated Germany had to compensate them for their losses. These reparations payments were so onerous that they helped destabilize Germany politically and economically throughout the 1920s and 1930s, and laid the foundations for Hitler's rise to power. This was predictable in June 1919, even as the ink dried on the Treaty of Versailles, which set out the punitive financial terms. Indeed, Keynes made his name with an outspoken pamphlet condemning the treaty, *The Economic Consequences of the Peace*.

"The Treaty includes no provisions for the economic rehabilitation of Europe," he warned.[1]

Looking at the inability of Germany and its allies even to feed their own populations, the victors of World War II chose a more enlightened path with Marshall Aid. The determination not to have history repeat itself in another twenty years' time led also to the creation of the international institutions that were the forerunners of today's EU and OECD. The latter—known until 1961 as the Organization for European Economic Cooperation (OEEC)—was then, as it remains now, a kind of economic brain trust for its member countries. These were to start with the Western European economies, joined later by Japan and subsequently by more countries as they graduated to "developed" economy status. In addition to directing the Marshall Aid funds, the OEEC took on the role of gathering national accounts figures for all the member countries and making comparisons among them. Today, international agencies, prominently the World Bank, publish GDP comparisons for all the countries in the world. These figures should allow us to answer questions such as: Has the Chinese economy overtaken the U.S. economy? Is Ghana a poor country or not? But—as already indicated—the answers are not as clear as you might think.

Nevertheless, the growth of real GDP is the single most important benchmark measure of how an economy is doing, and it was particularly important in the immediate postwar years. Was the Marshall Plan working?

Not only was it working, greatly helped by political and institutional reforms in the recipient countries, it ushered in three decades of strong growth and low inflation. Governments seemed able to direct the economy with some finesse, and many continued the planning they had begun during the years when they were mobilized for war. Unemployment was low. Although there were some obvious problems—be it a shortage of housing in the United Kingdom, or the need for rationing of food to continue for years after the end of the war—the foundations of prosperous modern consumer societies were being laid. The period is sometimes known in the English-speaking economics world as the postwar Golden Age. To the French, it is *les Trentes Glorieuses*. As with any golden age, some people look back on it with fond nostalgia and wonder why we can't return to that period when GDP seemed to do the bidding of government economic policymakers.

The Postwar Rebound

It is one of the distasteful aspects of a disaster that the immediate consequence is a boom in GDP growth. GDP does not measure the nation's assets or balance sheet, only its flow of income, expenditure, and production from year to year. Wipe out a portion of the assets, whether through natural or manmade disaster, and the activity or repairing and replacing will increase the growth of GDP. Exactly this pattern occurred after World War II. Table 2 shows real GDP growth

Table 2: Real Annual GDP Growth Rates (Percent)

Country	1950–1973	1973–1998
United States	3.93	2.99
United Kingdom	2.93	2.00
France	5.05	2.10
Germany	5.68	1.76
Japan	4.61	4.96

Source: Angus Maddison, *The World Economy: A Millennial Perspective* (Paris: Organization for Economic Cooperation and Development, 2000).

rates for the member countries of the OEEC in the postwar era compared with the subsequent twenty-five years. For a more recent comparison, the average annual real-terms growth rate for OECD countries in the first half of the 2000s—considered a boom period in recent economic history—was 2.5 percent on average.

Even though the business cycle—the periodic downs and ups of the economy as a whole—returned, GDP growth continued above its earlier rates during the 1950s, 1960s, and early 1970s. In the United States, GDP growth averaged nearly 4 percent a year from 1950 to 1973, compared with less than 3 percent a year between the two world wars. The United Kingdom's postwar 2.93 percent compares with just over 1 percent a year from 1913 to 1950.[2]

There is no simple explanation for the thirty-year success story, and it is probably a story in which politics matters as much as economics, given that it applies to the western democracies in that period.[3] One hypothesis, put forward in 1969 by Ferenc Janossy, was that the postwar economy had just been reverting to its pre-1914 trend, and when it had caught up to that trend, growth would slow again—as it later did.[4] Most economists prefer less fatalistic explanations, however, and divide the reasons for long-term growth into increases in the availability of resources (described as "factors of production")—mainly labor and capital—and improvements in the use of the available resources, or improved productivity. Both elements contributed to Golden Age growth. Particularly important was the continuously improving level of education among the workforce. In addition, a succession of new technologies became available and entered into wider use. A number of these were the fruits of military innovation. They included materials such as synthetic rubber and plastics.

They also included air travel, the first introduction of electronic computers into civilian use, improvements in radio communication, and many other innovations. By 1963, Harold Wilson, soon to become Britain's prime minister, was moved to talk about the "white heat" of the scientific and technological revolution, so thick and fast did new inventions seem to be arriving in everyday life.

Perhaps as important was the steadily improving availability of consumer goods, and the virtuous circle of consumer spending, increased output of consumer goods, increased employment, and higher incomes. The insight that it is important to have a prosperous consumer base and therefore pay good incomes in order to build a successful market for consumer products famously dates back to Henry Ford and his "motor car for the great multitude" produced from 1915 on. The phenomenon of mass consumerism came to life in the postwar years, however. Numerous products spread steadily to a growing proportion of households until by the 1970s they were almost ubiquitous: cars, radios, refrigerators, washing machines, TVs, cameras, lawnmowers, telephones ... the list is long. Nondurable goods followed: fashions, music, Elizabeth David or later Julia Child cookbooks, and dinner parties for friends. Teenagers were invented. With all the goods most of us own now, it is startling to look back over the decades and realize how recent consumerism is. For example, it wasn't until 1950 that 75 percent of U.S. households had a washing machine, and the same benchmark wasn't reached in Europe until 1970. Cars did not reach three-quarters of the U.S. population until about 1960. In the 1970s only half of U.K. or French households had a telephone; it was 94 percent or so of American households in the 1970s, but the European countries didn't catch up until the late 1990s. With some newer technologies, the pace has accelerated: it took only a decade for mobile phones to reach most Westerners, and the spread of smartphones with Internet access on the move is faster still.

How Well Are We Doing?

In July 1957, Harold Macmillan, Britain's prime minister, told his voters, in a phrase that became notorious when things started to go wrong soon afterward: "Most of our people have never had it so good." He was right, though. Living standards were the highest they had ever been, all kinds of new goods were available, and unemployment and inflation were low. With the war still fresh in everyone's memory, his statement was self-evidently true. But what about Germany, in particular, or even France, which had been occupied for most of the war? Had even Britain, despite its good 1950s, won the war only to lose the peace because of the enormous debts it incurred and the way it had been forced to gear the whole economy toward war production rather than normal investment?

In the United States, a different comparison was causing concern. Eisenhower's America enjoyed an even greater consumer boom than the European countries, symbolized by events like the appearance in 1950 of the first ever credit card, the Diner's Club card, and by the dawn of commercial TV advertising on the eve of the *Mad Men* era. World War II had given way to the Cold War and the arms race against the Soviet Union and its allies behind the Iron Curtain. The challenge to the United States and the West existed in the realm of ideas as well as troops, tanks, and nuclear missiles. Western consumerism was pitted against Soviet industry and technology.[5]

The communist countries had centrally planned economies, not market economies. Ministries in Moscow set the figures for the total number of all the items to be produced in the economy and cascaded that down to specific production quotas for different industries and individual factories. With the benefit of hindsight we can see that the idea that bureaucrats could possibly know enough in detail about a large, complex economy to plan it from the center successfully is ludicrous. In the early 1950s, in a much simpler economy than we have now, it was not obvious. The real shock to the United States came when the Soviet Union won the first stage of the space race with Yuri Gagarin's triumph in 1961 as the first human to go into space and orbit the Earth.

Which country was really ahead, the USA or the USSR? In order to make comparisons between any economies, a standardized measure is needed. GDP was the obvious one to use. Prior to 1940 a number of countries were calculating national income, using different definitions and adjustments. Immediately after the war the United States and the United Kingdom took the lead in coordinating the standardization of this measurement using the emerging framework of GDP and the national accounts. They did this through the United Nations. In 1947 the UN issued a technical report recommending how the calculations should be done—the appendix with the relevant detail was written by Richard Stone of the British Treasury. The OEEC followed up with guidelines published in 1951 and 1952, specifically for use in allocating Marshall Aid, and then the UN published the first official System of National Accounts in 1953 (abbreviated as SNA53). The communist countries followed suit but with their own national accounting standard in 1969, the Material Product System (MPS69). As noted in chapter 1, this had the significant difference that only physical goods counted while services were excluded, but in other respects it was an accounting framework similar to that for GDP.

Over the years, more and more countries have gathered and produced national accounts statistics, of an increasing degree of sophistication and detail. As Frits Bos remarks, "Nevertheless, still enormous differences in scope, detail, quality and frequency exist between the national accounts statistics published by countries."[6] In practice, only a few statisticians and economists concern themselves with the matters of detail. International organizations, mainly the OECD for the data on rich countries, and the World Bank and the IMF on all other countries, make sure that the statistics are as closely comparable as possible. Theirs are the figures that most economists will use when comparing how different economies are doing.

EXCHANGE RATES AND PURCHASING POWER

There is, though, one important hurdle, even when all the detailed questions about the collection of raw statistics and construction of the national accounts statistics have been dealt with. How are pounds or francs to be compared to dollars? The obvious answer is to use the exchange rate that prevailed between the two currencies at the time.

The obvious answer is too easy. It is only since 1973 that many exchange rates have been set by trading them in the international currency markets (some, especially China's, still are not). Prior to 1973, under the Bretton Woods system for managing international finance, the dollar-sterling exchange rate was fixed, at more than $4 to the pound sterling through World War II, but subsequently devalued to $2.80 and then $2.40. Suppose Americans were enjoying declining prices for something, say cars, which remained costly for British consumers. When exchange rates can adjust, the currency of a country with faster price increases will depreciate or weaken against the currency of the lower-inflation country. If that adjustment in the exchange rate cannot happen, a conversion of GDP from pounds to dollars will exaggerate the purchasing power of the higher-inflation United Kingdom. In the end, the pressures of keeping the exchange rate fixed proved too much, and weak currencies like the pound were officially devalued from time to time. Since then many exchange rates have found their own level in the currency markets. But that means that they are subject to sudden large fluctuations that are not linked to fundamental economic changes but rather to the whims of the financial markets. *uncertainty → fluctuate*

A trickier issue concerns the fact that only part of any country's output is traded at all. Much of it takes the form of services and goods sold within the country only. This includes large categories of spending, such as staple foods, and services like haircuts, retailing, water supply, education, funeral parlors, entertainment, and so on. In poor countries, the prices of services of this kind are often very low by Western standards, as anybody who has personal experience of the comparison from their travels will know. A conversion of GDP (which, of course, includes all these nontraded items) using market exchange rates (which depend on trade between countries) will be misleading, and possibly to a great extent for a low-income country that trades only a small proportion of its national output. What is needed is a conversion rate that takes account of these substantial differences in purchasing power when nontraded goods and services are taken into account.

It did not take long for this problem to become clear as statisticians and economists constructed GDP figures for more and more countries in the 1950s and 1960s. The solution was to construct "purchasing power parity" (PPP) exchange rates, which use data on *all* prices in the economy to adjust the actual exchange rate to one that reflects living standards more realistically. These rates are applied to convert GDP for every country into PPP dollars in the tables of international comparisons. The idea of purchasing power parity dates back to the early twentieth century and Colin Clark was the first person to try to calculate PPP conversion rates, in 1940. Further work continued alongside the development of national accounts after the war. The OEEC published the first PPP-adjusted GDP figures in 1954, based on the work of Milton Gilbert and Irving Kravis. Kravis started to extend the PPP rates to other countries, and established the International Comparison Project in 1968. He subsequently, with his colleagues Alan Heston and Robert Summers, created the Penn World Tables in 1978. This data set of international GDP tables came to be universally used by economists who wanted to compare growth rates and macroeconomic performance in different countries. It was recognized as an essential statistical resource, which the United Nations took charge of at first, and is now maintained and published by the World Bank in its International Comparison Project.

The use of PPP conversion rates, done unthinkingly by most economists, is controversial, however. Compared to converting every country's GDP to one currency using the prevailing market exchange rate, the PPP conversion factors will raise the relative level of GDP of those low-income countries where nontraded goods and services are cheap. That was, after all, the point of devising the purchasing power parity concept. But many critics think the PPP conversion ends up overstating the income of poor countries. Recent research confirms suggestions that the PPP approach understates the differences in living standards among different countries.[7]

The governments of low-income countries were concerned, however, that any adjustment that increased the (apparent) level of their GDP would make it less likely that they would get aid and cheap loans from the World Bank. Their level of need would appear lower with a PPP conversion than with an exchange-rate conversion of their GDP or GDP per capita. This matters: one example is that China's government is said to have persuaded the World Bank in 2000 to reduce its estimates of its GDP per capita in order to keep it below the threshold level for concessional loans.[8]

Some economists and other social scientists also challenge the price surveys used to calculate the PPP conversion factors. It is one thing to make the kind of adjustment required to compare the GDP of rich countries with well-established official statistical offices that are collecting price data for their own government's use. It is another matter entirely in a poor country where the quality of the statistics is low in general.

Many of the critics of PPP conversions also argue that there is an ideological bias, although usually entirely unconscious, in the process. Taking the PPP-based GDP comparisons on this basis at face value makes the trends in world poverty levels and income distribution look more encouraging than they really are. And if poverty has been declining rapidly, and inequality between countries not getting wider but if anything diminishing, as the comparisons suggest, then there is no reason to worry about the process of the globalization of international trade and investment that characterized the 1990s and 2000s. This is obviously a pretty fundamental question. Are the poorest countries getting less poor or not? To some extent the answer is obvious from the way everyday life in Chinese cities has visibly changed: there has certainly been a big increase in living standards for a large proportion of China's urban population, and that's enough to affect the global picture. Beyond that, though, the answer does depend on how the GDP of different countries is converted onto the same basis.

The statistical controversy has immense practical consequence: purchasing power parities are widely used to measure and compare living standards and economic performance around the world. They are the basis of almost every economic study looking at how countries grow. They determine policy choices made by national governments and international agencies.

To understand the issues, we need to go back to how the PPP conversion factors are worked out. There are, to start with, slightly different ways of constructing the conversion factors from the basic price data. Each individual country could have a PPP conversion rate worked out separately vis-à-vis the U.S. dollar, or all the conversion rates can be worked out simultaneously. In the latter case, you could choose either to give each country the same weight in the calculation, or to weight it by its size. Another decision is whether to do anything more complicated than adjusting price indexes in order to get at the underlying question of how to compare true living standards in different countries. The most commonly used PPP conversion factors used now involve different weights applied to national price indexes based on surveys of households in the different countries; these are called Geary-Khamis dollars.

What are the grounds on which this conventional approach can be challenged? They can be divided into the practical and the technical.

In the first case, the issue is what price surveys in low-income countries actually measure. The PPP conversion factors are based on large-scale international surveys used to benchmark prices in different countries. The most recent of these were carried out in 1985 (in 60 countries), in 1993 (in 110 countries), and in 2005 (in 143 countries). China's government refused to take part in either of the first two, so the statisticians made some informed guesses based on smaller available surveys covering urban areas. India's government refused to take part in the 1993 one, so the figures used instead were extrapolated from the 1985 results. The safe conclusion is that there is a margin of error in the PPP adjustments in the 1985 and 1993 exercises, and so also in comparisons based on them.[9] Both China, for the first time ever, and India took part in the 2005 survey, which covered 95 percent of the world's population. There remains a practical question about the quality of the data provided by each country; there are quite a lot of gaps that need to be filled by estimated figures. Setting aside that issue, though, the adjustments made as a result of the Chinese survey led the World Bank in 2007 to cut its estimate of China's real GDP in PPP terms by a staggering 40 percent. The Bank claimed the new estimates were better: "This is the first time China participated in the ICP. Previous estimates were extrapolated ... these extrapolations failed to take into account the change in structure and increase in prices over time." But the economist Surjit Bhalla pointed out that there were huge changes in the figures for many countries as a result of the 2005 surveys: "There are 21 countries with a higher negative GDP change (downgrading) than the −40 per cent for China; among these several large population economies like Ghana (−52 per cent), Nepal (−44), Bangladesh (−44), the Philippines (−43), and Uganda (−42 per cent). GDP in India has been reduced by 36 per cent." He added: "For the OECD economies, there is virtually zero difference as for most parts of the non-Asian world."[10] Even among the rich economies, though, the differences might matter; new PPPs based on 2011 data introduced by the OECD at the start of 2014 showed Mexico's economy measured this way to have become bigger than Canada's. And size matters in international politics.

Small wonder there is a good deal of suspicion of PPP calculations. The technical issue concerns the use of price indexes based on the survey data to adjust exchange rates and turn them into PPP conversion factors. The question the raw data should be used to answer is: "How much must the average expenditure in one country be increased to enable its typical inhabitant to have the same standard of living as a typical inhabitant of a richer country?" Simply using the normal method does not address this question. The economist Nicholas Oulton has used the same data as the World Bank in its International Comparison Program to calculate instead (using an econometric technique) what he describes as "true PPPs." Using these shows that "the standard of living in the poorest countries is now only about half the level estimated using the World Bank's PPPs."[11]

So there is nothing minor about the rather technical question of how to convert one country's GDP to the same basis as another country's, for the purposes of comparison. The results of the different methods of conversion—exchange rate, conventional PPP method using different kinds of weights to create the index used for adjustment, and "true PPPs"—can vary substantially. Take the comparison of GDP per capita in the United States and the Democratic Republic of Congo (DRC). In 2005, converting using the exchange rate suggested that a resident of DRC would need to be multiplied by 397 to achieve the same level of welfare or living standard as the typical U.S. resident. Using the World Bank's standard PPP conversion, the multiple would need to be 236; with other conventional types of PPP adjustment, it would be between 190 and 248; and with true PPPs, it would be between 380 and 502. We know DRC is a desperately poor country, and any catching up at all with living standards in the rich countries would be welcome. How far there is to go is not known, although perhaps that doesn't matter, given what we do know from other evidence about the two countries' relative living standards.

Both the International Comparison Program and alternative approaches to comparing GDP in different countries are—like creating GDP statistics in the first place—major efforts involving large statistical databases built from a patchwork of data sources of varying quality and timeliness. These are subsequently manipulated in technically demanding, complicated ways. There is no question but that economists will continue to use the World Bank data on GDP converted at purchasing power parity, on its methodology. Few people have either the expertise or the time to do anything else. The comparisons do provide useful information. But the large margin of uncertainty around this information should never be forgotten.

WHAT DID THE INTERNATIONAL COMPARISONS SHOW?

It would be easy to apply hindsight and superimpose what economists know now about international patterns of GDP growth over the decades since 1945 onto this description of how the raw material for those comparisons came to be assembled. But even as late as the mid-1970s, GDP data were available on a comparable basis, adjusted for purchasing power parity, for only a small number of countries. In the 1950s, when the economic theory of growth was in its early stages, the figures were available for just a few of the most developed economies. Early theories of how economies grow, and how the process of economic development occurs, set out by economists such as Roy Harrod and Evsey Domar, Robert Solow, and Paul Rosenstein-Rodan in the 1950s had little empirical evidence available with which to test their theories.

So it is not surprising that the theories, although expressed in the elegant algebra beloved of modern economists, were simple. Solow's model of growth remained the basic workhorse theory until the 1980s. It said that the economy's growth of its total output depended on the growth in the inputs needed—land or materials, labor and capital—and an unexplained remainder or residual labeled "technical progress." When applied to actual GDP data, the results were mildly embarrassing for the theory, because studies revealed that the great majority of postwar GDP growth was "explained" by the "technical progress," that is, by the one part of the theory that had no economic explanation. Technical progress was treated in this growth model as manna from heaven. Business investment created new capital to use in production. Labor grew by an increasing working-age population and, as the growth models became more refined, the increasing level of education and skill in the workforce. Both contributed to growth, but "technology" explained more.

These simple theories seemed to fit what was known about the recent experience of GDP growth around the world. The pattern of growth in the OEEC/OECD economies in the postwar decades clearly showed the dramatic catch-up by the devastated combatant countries and the *relative* decline in the United Kingdom (although it too grew at a rate that would later come to be regarded as a Golden Age phenomenon).

As for the comparison between the United States and its Cold War opponent, the USSR, it was some decades before the far less impressive growth of the planned economies became apparent. The Communist authorities did not have reliable statistics—every factory manager had a strong incentive, sometimes as strong as fear of the labor camps, to report excellent results, at least in line with the targets set by the central planning ministry. For Moscow did indeed plan a specific number for everything produced in the Soviet economy, with the central targets cascaded down to every factory and farm in the country. The targets for production were broad brush—number of pairs of shoes, volume of steel of different types. There was cheating. For example, a target could sometimes be achieved by putting a brick inside of a TV set, to report the weight of shipments out of the factory. Quantity targets meant that quality didn't matter. Eventually, however, central planning delivered weak growth even as recorded by the official statistics, and there was a chasm between the living standards of Western consumers and of people living behind the Iron Curtain. Matters were even worse in China, where the madness of Maoism led to mass famine, as well as the famous—or notorious—conformity in dress and behavior.

For those economies not distorted by central planning, the Solow model could account for the broad differences in performance between countries in terms of the increase in the use of the inputs or factors of production. The Marshall Aid–funded increase in investment succeeded brilliantly in achieving the Plan's aims of turning previously hostile and dreadfully impoverished nations into peaceful, prosperous trading partners. The United States' Marshall Plan remains one of the most visionary acts of statesmanship ever put into practice. And the postwar recovery fueled itself, becoming a virtuous circle of investment, technological discovery, and economic growth. Economists were confident that they knew how to use government spending and taxation to manage GDP, using the mechanics of the circular flow developed in the national accounts. But the Golden Age was not to last.

THREE

The Legacy of the 1970s:
A Crisis of Capitalism

When sorrows come, they come not
single spies, but in battalions.
William Shakespeare, *Hamlet*

After the postwar boom, Western capitalism started to falter, and its troubles were various. There were four distinct challenges to conventional economic thinking by the 1970s, challenges that corresponded to disturbing developments in the global economy.

The first was the switch from a virtuous circle of strong economic growth with steady prices to disappointing growth or even recession (when GDP declines for a sustained period, conventionally six months), combined with high and accelerating inflation. This ugly phenomenon had the ugly name *stagflation.* Conventional economic management tools seemed to make matters worse rather than better. Certainly there seemed no way to squeeze inflation down to tolerable levels without bringing about a serious recession. When the oil-producing countries in OPEC (the Organization of Petroleum Exporting Countries, dominated by Saudi Arabia and other Middle Eastern countries) then dramatically increased the price of oil in 1973 and again in 1975, recession was unavoidable.

The second challenge was the intensity of the Cold War. We tend now to think of the 1950s as being its height because of the political conformism of the McCarthy era, the Korean War, and the development of the insane but (as it turned out) correct theory of Mutually Assured Destruction. Yet the fact that it had persisted for twenty more years with no abatement was surprisingly demoralizing. Although it was clear to internal dissidents that the communist economies were failing, the disastrous results of central planning would not be understood in the West for another decade because of the publication of false statistics by the Soviet Union.

A third challenge came from the emerging environmental movement. In 1972 an influential report, *The Limits to Growth*, painted a gloomy picture of the costs of economic growth and an increasing population. It made the intuitively appealing (although, as it turned out, incorrect) argument that GDP growth, compounded year after year, would soon hit the limits of available natural resources. It predicted that *almost all* minerals and energy supplies would run out by 2070. The concept of "sustainability" entered the wider economic policy debate. The gloomiest environmental predictions of the time have not come true, because the doomsters ignored the realities of price changes and innovation affecting the use of resources, but the understanding that there may be a trade-off between environmental and economic aims is a lasting legacy of the environmental movement born in the 1970s.

Finally, by the 1970s most of the poor, developing economies had been free from colonial government for ten to
twenty years and their governments had received many millions of dollars in overseas aid (or rubles, if they were in the
orbit of the Soviet-bloc countries). Yet the confidence on
the part of development economists that the mechanics of
economic growth were understood had clearly proven mis-
placed. There were many factors that contributed to the fail-
ures of economic development, including the fighting of the
Cold War by proxy on the territories of these ex-colonies,
and the endemic corruption of their governments. In addition, though, a subtler understanding of what development
means came to replace the focus on the simple mechanics
of GDP and its components. Life expectancy, child mortality,
and access to education and to technologies such as electricity and communications came into focus instead—or, in other
words, welfare rather than output. This, too, has proven a
lasting challenge to the dominance of GDP.

It would be impossible to untangle each cause and effect,
but these four challenges to the by then conventional postwar economic framework came to a head at the same time,
the early 1970s. They coalesced into the most profound crisis
of capitalism since the Great Depression and until our own
Great Financial Crisis.

STAGFLATION

Nineteen sixty-eight was an iconic year. Young people fought
police or soldiers on the streets in the United States, France,
and Czechoslovakia (as it then was). Liberation movements
burst into flower around the world. It is not poverty and de-
spair that cause revolutionary activity in modern times, but

rather comfortable prosperity. Skipping school to hurl stones at the riot police and evade tear gas is a luxury indulged in only by young people who are not really worried about finding a job when they need one. Likewise, one can afford to experiment with drugs, free love, personal liberation, and self-discovery only in a prosperous economy. By 1968, there had been a quarter century of absolutely extraordinary growth.

The GDP figures give the scale: Western living standards had approximately trebled since 1950.[1] Unemployment had fallen to historic lows. There was a job for everybody who wanted one. A man could act as breadwinner for the whole family, reasonably secure in his job and well paid with a secure pension. The unemployment rate lay between 0.5 percent and 4 percent in the OECD's member countries in 1970 (compare this to between 4 percent in Switzerland and 25 percent in Greece and Spain in 2012).

To understand the true impact of postwar GDP growth, though, statistics alone are not enough to tell the story. Between 1945 and the late 1960s, the world had gained: dramatic new treatments for previously fatal or debilitating illnesses including smallpox and polio; famously, the contraceptive pill; affordable civilian air travel and the beginnings of the foreign holiday boom; color TV and telephones and modern domestic appliances in many homes; manmade fibers in clothes; Velcro; nylons. Even the most apparently trivial brought great increases in consumer welfare. For example, DuPont sold nearly eight hundred thousand pairs of nylon stockings on the first day they went on sale, 15 May 1940, and sixty-four million by the end of the first year. There was outrage among women when the supply dried up the following year due to the nylon yarn being diverted to war production.[2]

It is hard to exaggerate the significance of scientific and technological discoveries brought into everyday use during this era. Perhaps one example will make the wider point. Alexander Fleming first discovered penicillin in the laboratory in 1928. There were medical trials throughout the 1930s. In 1942, Merck's first commercial batch of the lifesaving antibiotic, a precious five and a half grams of it (half the entire stock of the United States) was used on a patient with streptococcal septicemia. By 1950, it was in mass production and its price had fallen to four cents a dose, the same as one-sixteenth of a gallon of milk.[3] It was not just that this flood of innovations existed but that so many people could afford them. As the economic historian David Landes observed, Nathan Meyer Rothschild, the richest man in the world of his time, died in 1836 for want of an antibiotic to cure an infection.[4]

This is what GDP growth consists of.

So what was going wrong by the late 1960s, a decade that ended with students in the streets throwing stones and crude Molotov cocktails at the police, workers on strike, power cuts, and citizens hoarding food?

As so often in life, the roots of failure lay in the nature of success. There was, in a way, too much growth. The tools of demand management proved too tempting and were used to boost the economy whenever there was a business cycle downturn. Both lower interest rates and extra government spending (or tax cuts) were generally used to try to limit downturns and keep the level of employment high. Politicians and other officials had in mind the model of the economy as a machine, just like the mechanical Phillips Machine that gave physical form to the circular flow of income in the national accounts (see chapter 1). Strong postwar growth seemed to validate their confidence; they overlooked the fact that *by design* GDP would increase when those policy levers were operated, at least in the short term. The definition of

GDP was constructed around Keynes's model of how the economy works. Besides, human nature and politics being what they are, it was rarer to find the tools of demand management being put into reverse gear during a business cycle boom until there was every sign of an economic crisis. People grew used to the experience of growth and confident about always having a job. They began to expect annual wage increases, an expectation reinforced as inflation started to go up. In unionized countries and industries, the unions did what they are supposed to and demanded higher pay for their members. In some countries, among them the United Kingdom, there were bruising battles between the unions, on the one hand, and the government and employers, on the other—with violent strikes that left shortages of food including bread as the bakers went on strike, mountains of rubbish on the streets, and frequent power cuts. As long as demand in the economy was strong, there was no reason for many employers not to agree to wage demands, as they could pass on higher labor costs in price increases to their customers, which in turn fueled more wage demands. The virtuous circle of confidence, investment, and growth in GDP flipped into a vicious spiral of expectations of rising wages and prices, and slow growth or recession. The oil price increases announced by OPEC after the Arab-Israeli war of 1973, leading to similarly large rises in the prices of other commodities, mixed into the stagflationary brew. The power of compound arithmetic means that the effect of a slower average growth rate cumulates quickly. At 4 percent a year (average U.S. growth in the 1960s), GDP will double in 17 years; at 3 percent a year, it will double after 24 years; at 2 percent a year, it will double only after 35 years. So a one percentage point slowdown in average annual growth, as in the 1970s, will be felt quickly.

The extraordinary turnaround in the economic situation in the Western democracies can be summed up by a relationship economists call the Phillips curve, after Bill Phillips, the economist who discovered it. In addition to building his famous machine, he noticed that, in the economic statistics for the United Kingdom for 1861 to 1957 there was a negative relationship between inflation and unemployment.[5] This empirical fact turned out to hold for other countries, too. It looked like a solid economic law that policymakers could exploit, just as they could make use of the multiplier in setting government spending and taxation. It seemed possible to choose a combination of unemployment and inflation. Many governments, especially ahead of an election, naturally preferred to tolerate a little bit more inflation to get unemployment down. Although voters don't like inflation because it reduces their spending power, adding extra jobs at the cost of a small increase in the rate of inflation has obvious appeal. The trouble was that as soon as governments started to try to choose the point they preferred on this trade-off between unemployment and inflation, the trade-off got worse. By the end of the 1970s, economists had concluded that the only lasting effect of trying to move along the Phillips curve would be to increase inflation, while the unemployment rate would go back to where it had started. They concluded that there was a "natural" rate of unemployment that depended on what incentive firms had to hire extra workers.[6] Trying to go below that by deficit spending would prove inflationary.

The dismal economic experience of the 1970s paved the way for both a revolution in thinking about the economy and a political revolution, too. In economic theory, there was a loss of faith in the simple Keynesian demand management tool of adjusting the government's budget deficit. Instead, the new consensus was that the government should concentrate on creating a good environment for business—low and stable taxes, labor market deregulation, and the new policy of privatization of formerly state-owned corporations in the United Kingdom, followed by other countries. And to keep inflation under control, the central bank should limit the growth of the money supply. But this new consensus lay ahead. In the 1970s, the economics profession was bitterly divided about macroeconomic policy. In 1975, the United Kingdom had 24 percent inflation and zero growth in real GDP, plus a balance of payments deficit so big that the IMF had to provide emergency finance the following year, just as it has recently for Greece and Iceland. It was the first time one of the world's leading industrial economies had needed to ask for this kind of bailout. In the United States the situation was little better, as its government had the strain of financing the Vietnam War and the Cold War arms race throughout the decade. In 1975, U.S. GDP declined while inflation rose to more than 10 percent. Almost all the OECD's member countries were facing stagflation, and for the first time in a generation economists were not confident they had the answers.

COMMUNISM

Every era is politically divided but it can be hard to recall the character of the division in an earlier time. From this side of November 1989, when the fall of the Berlin Wall symbolized the sudden, unexpected, and complete collapse of communism and its system of economic planning, it is easy to assume that those events were inevitable. That is not how it looked beforehand, not even when Margaret Thatcher and Ronald Reagan won their respective first election victories in 1979 and 1981, and certainly not in the 1970s. In 1970,

Stalin's crimes against his own people were known, but Mao's did not emerge for another decade. As for the economy, even expert analysts in the intelligence community who studied the figures did not realize the extent to which the statistics on communist-bloc economic output were fictitious. Indeed, while the Americans spied on the Soviets to get economic intelligence, the Soviets also spied on the CIA's estimates of their own economy. The fabrication was spread through the economy. Individual factories were set output targets by the planning ministry. These were expressed in terms of volume—number of TV sets or pairs of shoes—or even weight. Targets of this kind are easy to meet. It doesn't matter what the shoes are like, whether they are durable, comfortable, in the right sizes for the majority of wearers, or stylish. It doesn't matter whether the TV sets work after six months or if the panel at the back constantly falls off. Combined with the amount of investment in heavy industry, the military, and prestige projects, the ambitious economic plans therefore delivered impressive output growth statistics—the figures being those for Net Material Product rather than GDP (NMP was about three-quarters the level of GDP at the time of the collapse of communism).

What the official Soviet statistics showed at the time was national output growing at rates better than in the West: 5.7 percent a year in the first half of the 1970s, 4.3 percent a year in the second half, and these were slower growth rates than had been reported in the 1960s.[7] So few Westerners traveled behind the Iron Curtain, and fewer still in China, that the obviously lower standard of living there was not widely experienced. There was an odd psychological disconnect between the widespread knowledge that the people of Eastern Europe thirsted for blue jeans and pop music, the most blatant symbols of Western consumerism, and the natural conclusion that ought to have pointed to about the state of the communist economies. Perhaps the explanation lay in the emerging crisis in the capitalist economies. Calling in the IMF, as the United Kingdom had done, did not set the stage for any Western triumphalism.

On the contrary, the left-right divide grew bitter in the 1970s. The liberation movements emerging from the individualism of the previous decade were increasingly angry, occasionally even violent. Revolutionary politics were fashionable—one of the best-selling posters of the era, adorning many student walls, was the iconic black and red image of Che Guevara. Academics dived down the long dead end of Marxist-inspired critical theory, only now fizzling out in university departments. Organized labor became far more militant. There were more and more strikes, even in the far less militant United States. In fifteen industrial countries other than the United States, the number of days per worker lost due to strikes was 1,641 in the 1960s, 2,586 in the 1970s, 1,632 in the 1980s, and a mere 658 in the 1990s.[8] These helped bring about the Reagan and Thatcher victories, and the subsequent policy reaction, including tough restrictions on the right to strike. But that, again, uses hindsight. For a decade, it looked as though the capitalist system was the one that was broken.

ENVIRONMENTALISM

The Earth viewed from space: it is one of the most memorable and beautiful images in human history, our blue planet. The first image of this kind was taken by the astronaut William Anders from Apollo 8 in 1968. Did the new perspective it gave us trigger a sense of responsibility, of stewardship for the planet? Perhaps.

Between 1945 and 1970, world GDP increased threefold, after adjusting for inflation. The world's population rose from 2.5 billion to 4 billion over the same period. It was a truly dramatic increase in the average standard of living, although very much confined to the rich "club" of countries. In 1970, there were twenty-two of these (there are thirty-four OECD member countries now). For the first time, concerns about the effect of the economic growth on the environment and the planet as a whole started to emerge.

Some of this concern grew out of local events. For example, in the United States the publication of Rachel Carson's *Silent Spring* in 1962, about the effect of pesticide use on bird populations, is credited as one of the early seeds of the environmental movement. The Cuyahoga River in northern Ohio caught on fire in 1969, spurring a number of environmental measures including the 1972 Clean Water Act (with limited impact, the Love Canal scandal later in the 1970s would suggest). But there was a new tide of concern about the global environment, the big picture, in other Western countries, too. Seeing the Earth from space had given us a vivid new perspective. Perhaps prosperity itself created the opportunity to reflect on the effects of growth. After all, it is not until income reaches a level comfortably above paying for food, housing, and clothes, and is enough to give people ample leisure time and the opportunity to read and debate, that many would worry about anything beyond the slog of day-to-day life.

The sheer growth of numbers and the resources used by the growing population prompted a famous diatribe, *The Population Bomb*, by Paul Ehrlich. The book caused a splash on publication in 1968, with its gloomy predictions. But Ehrlich subsequently lost a bet with the economist Julian Simon of the University of Maryland. In 1980, Simon bet Ehrlich that the price of any five commodities he cared to nominate would have declined (adjusted for general inflation) by the end of ten years. Simon was relying on his economist's reasoning that if something became scarce because of the growing pressure of demand, its price would increase relative to everything else, and that would encourage people both to limit their use of it and to find alternatives. So the combination of rationing by price and innovation would provide an automatic market mechanism to correct for shortages. Ehrlich chose the five metals he thought would run out soonest, whose prices would therefore rise fastest. He was wrong: all the prices had indeed fallen at the end of the decade. This well-known example illustrates the contrasting types of analysis that still characterize many disagreements about whether economic growth is or is not bound to damage the environment. People who see an unavoidable trade-off between higher GDP and environmental harm tend to extrapolate from current adverse trends. Economists like Julian Simon believe that people's behavior changes in a self-correcting way when adverse trends go far enough, as they respond to price signals. Drawing up a balance sheet for the effect of two and a half centuries of modern economic growth on the global environment is a tall order, as there has obviously been a profound impact in many dimensions, from the composition of the atmosphere to biodiversity to pollution to resource use. Chapter 6 will return to the question of whether, in GDP, there is a good enough measure of the sustainability of growth.

The outcome of the Ehrlich-Simon bet lay in the future. The new interest in environmental sustainability, reflected by *The Limits to Growth* report and other influential books, was itself limited. For the emerging economic crisis of the 1970s meant that policymakers in practice paid scant attention to the new environmental movement. The environmental movement was one of the strands of radical or left-wing politics, almost another kind of identity politics. The enormous jumps in the price of oil had the effect of leading to a permanent switch to less energy-intensive methods of production in industry, to the introduction of building methods involving better insulation, and to interest in renewable forms of energy generation. Besides, voters were far more interested in getting GDP back on track to grow than in its intangible consequences for the environment. Clean-air legislation and more fuel-efficient cars satisfied most people's pressing environmental concerns, whereas economic growth meant jobs and improving living standards.

Nonetheless, the concept of *sustainable* economic growth was born in the 1970s and has become ever more important as statistics on the many dimensions of environmental quality have joined statistics on the economy as important measures of human activity and well-being.

HUMAN DEVELOPMENT

In contrast to the OECD countries at the start of the 1970s, GDP per capita elsewhere in the world had not improved so much since 1945. There were, of course, mixed fortunes. Japan had rebounded dramatically from its wartime devastation, initially shepherded in important ways by the Occupation administration of General Douglas MacArthur. It was particularly successful in the mass production of (initially) cheap and cheerful consumer electronics. "Made in Japan" in the 1960s had the same kind of ring as "Made in China" in the 1990s. In 1964 Japan graduated into the OECD, and progressed to develop a sophisticated and high-quality industrial base that was more than a match for most other Western economies; now, only Germany rivals Japan for strength in manufacturing. A few other countries that were poor in the 1970s have since followed a similar path. In Europe, the low-income fringe—Italy first, then Ireland, Spain, and Portugal, and finally Greece—caught up a long way toward the high-income core. (How real or durable that catch-up has been is an open question at the moment, in the aftermath of the financial crisis.) A cluster of countries in Southeast Asia have enjoyed so-called economic miracles too, South Korea being the most prominent. The OECD's list of members has expanded from the OEEC's original eighteen countries to thirty-four today.

That leaves a lot of countries in the world that have never experienced the economic growth we take for granted. Average GDP per capita was $41,225 in 2011 in the high-income OECD countries and just $569 in the low-income countries, using the World Bank's classifications (all converted at PPP rates). But is the level of GDP per capita the best way to make the comparison between rich and poor? The question has all the more force because of the intense efforts over the decades to trigger GDP growth in developing countries. It is a thankless task to try to estimate the total amount of development aid paid by the taxpayers of rich countries to the governments of poor countries, but the figure would be in the trillions of dollars. The amount donated privately through international nongovernmental organizations dedicated to fighting poverty is another large figure. Yet GDP has not grown much for most of the postwar era in sub-Saharan Africa, and poverty remains widespread.

Mahbub Ul Haq, a Pakistani economist working at the World Bank in the 1970s and 1980s, and later (after a stint as Pakistan's finance minister) at the United Nations, introduced an alternative approach to measuring poverty and welfare. The indicator he launched, the Human Development Index

(HDI), built on the idea of measuring capabilities rather than income. The economist Amartya Sen, who subsequently won the Nobel Memorial Prize, had electrified the world of development economics with the argument that famines had nothing to do with income and poverty; rather, they were caused when governments were not responsive to the needs of their people, and in particular when there were no newspapers or broadcasters with sufficient independence to challenge and criticize government decisions. Democracies did not suffer famines, at any level of GDP per capita.[9] Sen went on to argue that although income per capita was important, it was not as complete a measure of people's welfare as their capabilities—this would include income or command over resources but also variables such as health, education, women's freedom, and access to key technologies such as electricity and roads.[10] The HDI measures these separate indicators and combines them into a single ranking. This is published every year by the United Nations Development Program. The same group of countries are at or near the top each year: Norway, Australia, New Zealand, the United States, Canada, other Scandinavian countries, and the Netherlands. Likewise, a group of conflict-ridden and/or landlocked countries are to be found near the bottom—DRC, Niger, Chad, and Burundi. But GDP per capita isn't everything in this index. My own country, the United Kingdom, has high GDP per capita but, at twenty-eighth in the HDI ranking, is surprisingly close to Greece or Slovakia, with much lower GDP per capita.

There is a positive correlation between GDP and the components of the HDI. Richer countries are able to afford better health care, to keep children in school and university for longer, and so forth. Conversely, healthier and better-educated people contribute to economic growth. So the virtuous circle of growth is evident in these figures. But the correlation between the level of GDP per capita and human development is not perfect. This is because they are measuring different things. GDP is measuring output and income, which are clear concepts despite the many difficulties involved in turning them into actual statistics. Human development is an indicator of welfare. This distinction needs to be borne in mind later, when we visit more recent suggestions for alternatives to GDP. Ironically, those people who argue most strongly for using an alternative to GDP for the developed economies tend to be focused on income and poverty measures above all else when it comes to developing countries.

The difference between GDP per capita and human development does matter for how you assess the efforts to assist developing countries, all those trillions of dollars in aid. The results in terms of GDP have been disappointing. The gap between incomes per capita of the world's poorest and richest countries has soared in the past half century. But in many other ways—the indicators included in the HDI—there is good news. The gap between rich and poor countries in terms of life expectancy and infant mortality has narrowed significantly, despite the scourge of HIV/AIDS in sub-Saharan Africa. Access to education has improved substantially in poor countries. Although the picture on the availability of technologies is mixed, there has been great progress in some areas: 47 percent of India's 246.6 million households still do not have indoor toilets or clean running water, but 63 percent have access to mobile phones, helping people get work more easily or get better prices for their produce in the markets. Life expectancy around the world is converging, with life expectancy even in many low-income countries now at seventy years. Infant mortality has fallen around the world, and fallen much faster in poor countries than in rich ones.[11]

This is to run ahead of the story, though. The point here is that the thinking behind the HDI was sowing another seed of doubt about the machinery of GDP and its management. The conventional way of thinking had broken down at home in stagflation the previous decade; and it was breaking down in what was then often still called the Third World as injections of aid spending had clearly failed to increase growth and GDP. And at the same time that postwar prosperity looked inherently fragile, or even unattainable in much of the world, the environmental costs of GDP growth were coming to the fore.

FOUR

1995 to 2005: The New Paradigm

It was no surprise that the crisis of capitalism in the late 1970s led to a reaction, both political and intellectual, against the Golden Age conventions. The clearest example came in the United States and the United Kingdom with the Reagan-Thatcher revolution. Reagan and Thatcher's policy agenda consisted of breaking the power of organized labor, deregulating the economy to encourage business, and privatizing state-owned corporations and other assets (including selling local authority housing to its tenants in the United Kingdom). Raising and lowering government spending and tax rates was no longer seen as the way to manage the economy's growth rate. It would bring only short-term results, at the long-term cost of more inflation and less investment. To improve growth and levels of income in a lasting way, the "supply side" of the economy needed to be more efficient, less restricted by unnecessary regulations. This menu of policy choices was mirrored by the development of a new consensus in economics, which also downplayed the scope for activist fiscal policy and instead emphasized the role of the central bank in providing monetary stability. The realization that the Phillips curve trade-off had grown worse over time and the experience of stagflation both made it plain that economists needed to change their views about how the economy as a whole worked.

Within a relatively short time, the polarization of views among economists that had marked the turbulent 1970s— between Keynesians and monetarists—gave way to a more or less monetarist consensus. For all our faults, economists do pay attention to evidence. But until relatively recently, there was very little evidence on which economists could base their views about how economies grow. The number of countries for which GDP data were available increased slowly, and had reached only sixty as late as 1985. For many of these, the data were of poor quality. Very few countries indeed had GDP data going back beyond the mid-1950s. Even those that had been gathering some kind of national income statistics for a long period did not have data series that were consistent over time because the definitions had changed so much. Thirty years' worth of annual data for sixty countries is not much when it comes to testing detailed causal explanations of growth, especially with one year's figures similar to the previous year's (because GDP and its components do not change much over time—the norm is a change of 1–3 percent a year).

UNDERSTANDING GROWTH

Even so, as more and more countries' GDP statistics became available, the theories of growth were refined from the Solow model, which placed so much weight on the important but unexplained role of technology. A new generation of growth models developed from the 1980s onward were able to start explaining how "technology" happened, rather than treating it as a mysterious "black box." In these "endogenous growth" theories, technological progress fed into GDP growth in a virtuous circle, because faster growth enabled more investment and innovation. "Technology" takes the form of ideas in people's minds, or education and skills, or ideas embodied in equipment and products. Looking explicitly at the importance of variables measuring education levels and levels of innovation such as patenting in business confirmed their role in explaining the difference in growth rates among different countries.

This empirical work based on postwar data was augmented by historical studies using data on GDP for a range of countries going back to the year 1000. Angus Maddison was an economic historian based at Groningen University in the Netherlands. His extraordinary International Comparisons Project undertook the immense task of finding from a wide range of historical sources all the raw statistics needed to construct GDP, on its modern definition, backward through history. Maddison, who died in 2010, was not well known outside the profession. But it is not an exaggeration to say that the data set he created is now an essential resource for economists studying macroeconomics and growth. After all, new technologies take very many years to go from bright idea in the laboratory or workshop to commercially viable product in widespread use—according to the economic historian Paul David, it is typically fifty years or longer. His example is the electric motor, which transformed factories and made assembly-line production possible. The fundamental inventions in electricity dated back to the 1870s, but it was not until the 1920s that most U.S. factories used electric power.[1]

It is not possible to explore these dynamics of innovation without having long runs of economic statistics. Maddison provided these. They were published only from 1999 on.[2] This means that until just over ten years ago, economists trying to explain growth were really flying blind. It must be said that economists now use Maddison's statistics blithely, without the due caution required. After all, to construct one thousand years of GDP data involved a lot of assumptions and clever guesswork. As we've seen, the conceptions of national income used before World War II were different, so Maddison had to project back a modern concept onto whatever data he found. Other historians take a strikingly different view of certain periods and countries. So the Maddison data set is convenient for looking at growth patterns across countries and over time—there is nothing else like it—but it should not be taken as definitive.

In a classic example of historical serendipity, the ability to look empirically at how technology brings about economic growth coincided with a period when a new technology was starting to spread so widely that it seemed bound to boost the economy. This was, of course, the computer and Internet revolution. This provides a good example of the kind of time lags Paul David described. The electronic programmable computer was one of the basic innovations of World War II. It emerged from the wartime code-breaking work at Bletchley Park in the United Kingdom and the brilliant conceptual leaps made by Alan Turing, and, across the Atlantic during and after the war, from the work of John Von Neumann and others involved in the development of nuclear weapons. Computers began as military and academic machines, then came into use in big businesses, and in the 1980s finally became small and cheap enough to spread to all offices and gradually individual homes. Separately, the communications protocols between computers were developed in the United States in the 1970s, by DARPA (the Defense Advanced Research Projects Agency) among other groups. Computer-to-computer communication spread through the academic world first, from the mid-1970s onward, but Internet use required quite a high level of special knowledge through the 1980s. Tim Berners-Lee made the Internet accessible to all with his invention of the World Wide Web, working at the CERN laboratory in Geneva, which had the first website online in 1991. "This is for everyone," as he put it.[3] The Web started to get ordinary users online in the mid-1990s, and twenty years later being online is almost ubiquitous in developed countries and spreading rapidly in developing countries. This latter trend is thanks in large part to mobile telephones and smartphones. Because separately, telecommunications technology has been revolutionized by a sequence of innovations such as fiber-optic cables, and in particular mobile telephony and other wireless communications. This epoch of the information and communications revolution has spanned forty years.

THE NEW ECONOMY BOOM

It was obvious by the mid-1980s that a lot of businesses were buying and using computers, but what effect this was having on the economy was not at all apparent. Robert Solow wrote a frequently quoted *New York Times Book Review* article in 1987 claiming, "You can see the computer age everywhere but the productivity statistics."[4] In fact, it took the convergence of a number of separate streams of technological innovation, plus the investment in new computer and communications equipment, plus the reorganization of businesses to use these new tools, before any benefit in terms of productivity or GDP could occur. For example, Wal-Mart is the leading example of how a business can transform its productivity using these technologies. McKinsey estimated that Wal-Mart on its own accounted for a substantial proportion of the pickup in American productivity in the late 1990s.[5] To achieve this, the company developed a model of sourcing goods from China and other low-cost countries, through an extremely sophisticated logistics operation, and retailing the goods in massive out-of-town stores. It was a radical reinvention of retailing. Studies of businesses investing in computer and communications equipment in the United States in the 1990s and 2000s indicate that without restructuring the business, productivity gains are small. But those that do restructure experience very large improvements in productivity.[6]

A decade after Solow's skeptical article, the computer revolution was beginning to be seen in the economy, at least in the United States. A recession in the early 1990s gave way to the longest period of expansion in GDP the United States had seen since the dawn of capitalism. There were only two quarters (in 2001) when GDP declined, slightly, between 1991 and 2007. In other countries there was a similarly long expansion, although with a less stellar rate of growth than in the United States. The growth of GDP always varies from year to year, but it is possible to abstract from this by looking at the averages for longer periods. Economists try to calculate the *potential* growth rate, looking at how fast the supply of labor and capital are growing and how productively they are being used. The average growth of productivity in the United States climbed from an annual average of 1.38 percent in 1972–1996 to 2.46 percent in 1996–2004.[7] Estimates for the potential U.S. growth rate rose dramatically from less than 2 percent a year to more than 3 percent a year according to the most optimistic views. In case this change sounds small, remember the power of compound arithmetic, this time operating favorably: at 2 percent a year, GDP will double after thirty-five years; at 3 percent a year after only twenty-four years. The new technologies were shaping up to outdo the Golden Age of the immediate postwar years if this continued.

Suddenly, everyone was talking about the New Economy or the New Paradigm. The new technologies seemed to have made possible a lasting increase in the productivity of the economy. Prominent among the enthusiasts was Alan Greenspan, then the long-serving chairman of the Federal Reserve Board. His judgment about the economy's potential growth rate was crucial because it was his job to use interest rates and monetary policy to choke off growth in demand that would prove inflationary. But there was no need to worry about inflation if the economy now had more *potential* to grow faster thanks to the new technologies, and therefore could easily satisfy the additional demand. In his memoir *The Age of Turbulence*, Greenspan describes his first discussion in 1995 with his Fed colleagues of the possibility of a "paradigm change" in the economy: "I've been looking at business cycles since the late 1940s. There has been nothing like this," he told them. "The depth and persistence of such technological changes appear only once every fifty or one hundred years."[8]

He was right—and then he was wrong. From today's side of the financial crisis, the New Economy hype looks almost delusional. In the United States and elsewhere, GDP grew slowly, if at all, for five years after the crisis and the rate of growth of productivity slowed correspondingly. Subsequently, some economists have concluded that we are in for a period of 'secular stagnation,' with no return to rapid, technology-driven productivity growth.[9] For a decade from the mid-nineties to the mid-noughties, though, all the evidence was stacking up in favor of a lasting change for the better in the economy, even looking at the published statistics for GDP. And there was every reason to believe that these were *understating* the actual rate of growth, perhaps significantly.

Measuring Services

Even before the new wave of technologies raised doubts about how well GDP reflects innovation, there were some troublesome difficulties in measuring parts of the economy. These included large parts of the service sector. Remember that the origin of GDP was the need to measure the use and availability of material resources in the economy at a time when these were severely constrained. Although there are complexities, it is reasonably straightforward to measure physical products. Raw data on the services sector of the economy have always been scarcer. As discussed earlier, Adam Smith believed services to be inherently unproductive and there was no need to account for them. Colin Clark in his early work on the nascent GDP statistics in the 1930s complained about the difficulty of finding raw data on service activities. The legacy of the Industrial Revolution was a lot of data on output of cotton and coal, and little counting of services. Yet even in 1937, the service sector accounted for just under half the jobs in the British economy and a similar proportion of the U.S. economy.[10]

Services also pose some challenges for the national accounts statisticians. Nominal GDP measures the amount purchased by final users in dollars or pounds, at market prices. For private-sector services this is straightforward, but not so for public-sector services. If these compete directly with the private sector, then prices in the private sector can some-times be used to value them. If there is no private-sector comparator, or the market is not truly competitive, the only alternative is to measure the value of these services in terms of the wages paid to the public-sector employees providing them. That gives a serviceable figure to use for GDP, but the catch is that those particular services by definition can never show any improvement in the amount of output per govern-ment employee. Many governments worry about poor pro-ductivity performance in public services, but in some cases they may be overlooking this statistical factor.

This worry about productivity in public services raises a deeper question, however. As the word suggests, productiv-ity is related to products. It measures number of units of out-put per unit of inputs. The main input in a service business is the time spent by the employees on their job. What is the output of a teacher, though? Number of children processed through the school? The average grade they attain on leav-ing? The highest subsequent qualification the children attain on average, or perhaps their lifetime earnings? Or even the quality of life those children subsequently enjoy, having been equipped at school for meaningful work and a fulfilling fam-ily life, along with an enjoyment of music or sport? Should we only bother to measure patients' health outcomes in some way? Is a hairdresser's productivity just the number of hair-cuts, or the premium he can charge because of the quality of his cuts or ambience of the salon?

These are, of course, unanswerable questions. The concept doesn't really fit. Yet services account for more than two-thirds of GDP in the OECD economies. There are additional vexing issues when it comes to financial services in particu-lar, a topic to which chapter 6 will return.

THE EXPLOSION OF VARIETY

A seemingly separate issue, also of increasing salience, is that the way GDP is measured makes it impossible to capture fully the effect of innovation. Innovation is constant, but in the 1990s it was apparent that a new wave of products and services based on information and communications technologies was starting to feature significantly in the spending of businesses and consumers.

Why does GDP not measure innovation well? Brad DeLong, the University of California–Berkeley economic historian, has given the example of successive innovations in lighting the home. There was a progression from expensive, smoky tallow candles, rarely used and giving out little light and much smoke, in the preindustrial era, to kerosene lanterns, to gas lighting, to modern electric lights at the touch of a switch. In the 1500s, most people went to bed whenever it grew dark, so expensive was the poor-quality light available to them. By the 1990s, you could go on holiday leaving the lights on by accident, and realize your mistake with only a mild pang of annoyance. Over the decades and centuries, the price of a lumen or unit of light fell dramatically. At the same time, the quality of lighting increased profoundly.[11] The raw statistics that go into the estimates of GDP—the number of candles bought or the number of light bulbs and lamps—never fully captured the scale of either the decline in price or the improvement in quality. According to William Nordhaus, in a famous study, conventional measurement had overestimated the price of light, and underestimated the real output, by a factor of between 900 and 1,600 since the beginning of the nineteenth century. If true of other technologies where there was rapid advance, this would add up to a significant underestimate of real growth in the GDP statistics.

What is true of this one item of consumer spending is true across the entire economy. Modern GDP growth is a story of continuing innovation and an explosion in variety. It has been rather fashionable to claim there is "too much" choice. The evidence points the other way. Econometric estimates of the value consumers derive from additional varieties of certain products, say of cereals, or book titles, indicate that this is large even for seemingly trivial innovations like apple cinnamon flavor Cheerios.[12] What must the benefit be when adding together everything from minor innovations in cereals, toothpastes, and flavors of tea, through more obviously novel innovations such as Velcro fastening or hybrid cars, to those we normally think of as high-tech, like smartphones and tablet computers, genetically targeted pharmaceuticals, and new materials such as graphene?

The question of how to account in GDP for dramatic changes in quality and declines in price became particularly acute in the case of computers by the mid-1990s. In the space of ten years, we had moved from a relatively small number of early adopter consumers with their Apple Lisas or Macintoshes to widespread ownership of more powerful home computers, including rapidly growing Internet use at home, plus increasingly widespread use of mobile phones; and in another ten years again to very widespread purchases of laptops, followed by tablets and smartphones. Each wave of these information and communications technologies saw the most rapid diffusion to date in a new technology. The other side of the coin to this rapid spread in use was the rapid decline in price. William Nordhaus calculated the speed at which the prices of a standardized unit of computer power had been declining: "Performance in constant dollars or in terms of labor units has improved since 1900 by a factor in the order of 1 trillion to 5 trillion, which represent compound growth rates of between 30 and 35 percent per year for a century." Official statistics understated the decline in prices because they did not take adequate account of improvements in the performance of computers, he argued.[13]

This question was investigated by a group of experts in the United States, the Boskin Commission. As discussed earlier, its 1996 report concluded that by failing to take account of the quality changes in goods such as computers, cameras, and phones, the U.S. Consumer Price Index had been overstating the rate of inflation by 1.3 percentage points a year, and correspondingly understating real GDP growth by compensating for phantom price increases. What appeared to be rising prices (or less rapidly declining prices) in fact reflected massive improvements in quality and in the benefits consumers derived from these goods. The findings of the Boskin Commission gave Alan Greenspan and the Federal Reserve more confidence about the economy's potential growth than they might otherwise have had. The other consequence of the commission's report was that statistical agencies in the United States and elsewhere increasingly turned to the use of what is known as "hedonic" price indexes in calculating the general price index to turn dollar GDP figures into a real-terms measure.

Hedonic is derived from the Greek word for things relating to pleasure. The aim of a hedonic index is to take account of quality changes in order to figure out the true price of the underlying benefit to the user. To calculate the hedonic price of a computer is to seek the price of certain characteristics that are bundled up in a computer. The statisticians take the actual price paid for personal computers of all kinds, and also gather data on the different characteristics of the machines people are buying. What is their memory size? Screen size and resolution? Do they have built-in Wi-Fi? The actual price is then regressed on these various characteristics—that is, an estimated equation is derived to find the coefficients that link the price paid to each type of feature. Any part of the price increase unrelated to specific improvements in the various qualities of the computer is a measure of inflation—in other words, an increase in price that has no grounding in quality improvements. This process is applied to a number of high-tech goods. The result was an increase in the estimated level of U.S. GDP and its growth over some years, although other countries subsequently "caught up" when they began to adopt the same technique. Other countries, including the United Kingdom, Canada, and Japan, have subsequently followed suit in calculating hedonic prices for such goods.

A second change made in the U.S. statistics at the same time had the same kind of effect. That was to switch to counting purchases of software by companies as a form of investment rather than a purchase of an intermediate good as it had been. In other words, software was no longer to be treated as a purchase between companies like components or stationery, to be netted out of the final sales figure to go into GDP; but instead as the purchase of something like a new machine or factory that would depreciate in value but also deliver a return over time. This methodological change was a bit controversial. Software tends to have a much shorter life than a machine installed on a production line, perhaps two years rather than ten, so it is not obviously the same kind of durable purchase. There is no sharp line between purchases of different types of software by businesses and by consumers for personal use. For example, many small and medium businesses might go to Staples or another big-box store to buy accounting software packages, whereas a big corporation would go direct to the vendor. So collecting the correct kind of raw data is a challenge. Finally, there is an overlap between the software sitting on a computer and the performance characteristics of the computer, so there is a risk that adopting both hedonic pricing and software as an investment double-counts the quality improvements. Nevertheless, official statistical bodies now treat business purchases of software as investment spending.

The consequence of introducing hedonic pricing and software as an investment was that real GDP seemed to be growing strongly by the late 1990s and early 2000s. The economy was booming, so the message from the GDP figures was not false. But the change may well have given the impression of a greater acceleration in growth than was the case. What's more, because the United States was the first country to switch to hedonic pricing for goods of this kind, it certainly made the American economy look stronger than its comparators in Europe or Japan. On the European side of the Atlantic, there was a good deal of agonizing among economic policymakers: computers were available for any business in any country to use, so why did the productivity benefits of the computer revolution appear to be confined to the United States? On the American side, there was a sense of triumphalism about the superiority of the U.S. economy and its "New Paradigm," with its Silicon Valley heroes and soaring stock market. Shocks like the 1995 Mexican near-default, the 1997–1998 Asian financial crisis and the collapse of Long Term Capital Management, and even the technology stock crash of 2001 and the horrors of 9/11 that year, were shrugged off after brief periods of crisis management. The economy appeared to be strong enough to weather anything, and GDP continued to expand for years to come, after a mild and brief downturn in 2001.

The questions about GDP raised by the New Economy episode still stand. GDP has never measured service-sector activity well, and services have been growing constantly as a proportion of what we spend our money on. Equally, GDP has never captured the most striking and important characteristic of modern capitalism, namely that it is an "innovation machine."[14] A better metric than the *size* of the economy might well be the *variety* of goods and services available. Research published in 2001 indicated that this variety had been increasing by an astounding 1 percent a year for forty years in the United States, and at an accelerating pace.[15] The invention of GDP predates this explosion in variety and does not begin to measure the benefits except in the few categories of goods to which hedonic pricing techniques are applied. These two shortfalls in measurement by GDP have converged because a good part of the growth in services since around 1980 has been accounted for by the business and professional services category, including entirely new activities linked to the information and communications sector. In a book published in 1996 I noted the phenomenon that growth in GDP for more than a decade had literally not weighed anything: all the incremental value-added growth was in intangibles of one kind or another.[16] A measure of the national economy designed for tangible, physical products only is not really a good measure of an increasingly weightless economy.

The lesson to draw from this discussion is that GDP is not, and was never intended to be, a measure of welfare. It measures production. As we saw in chapter 1, Simon Kuznets, one of the pioneers of national accounting, was keen to develop a measure of economic welfare. But the demands of wartime meant his ambition was overtaken by the need to measure production and productive capacity, in order to use scarce material resources and labor as efficiently as possible.

If the aim instead is to develop a measure of national economic welfare, we shouldn't be starting with GDP. Which suggests that any kind of amendment to GDP—whether hedonic pricing or the more radical alternatives suggested by critics of GDP discussed in the next chapter—is trying to turn it into something it was never designed for.

FIVE

Our Times: The Great Crash

A Greek Tragedy: Hubris, Ate, and Nemesis

There are three elements to classic Greek tragedy: arrogance, foolishness, and destruction: *hubris*, *ate*, and *nemesis*. These have played out around the world since the start of the financial crisis in 2008.

The arrogance was the triumphalism about the prevailing model of economic growth. It was based on technological innovation, of course, but also on financial market deregulation and the broader ideology of "free markets," and the globalization of finance and trade. As globalization expanded its reach and scope during the 1990s and 2000s it also generated opposition to what many campaigners saw as adverse and unacceptable side effects. The main focus of their criticism was the increase in global inequality as GDP per capita in the richest countries pulled ahead of the figure for the very poorest countries, most of which were to be found in sub-Saharan Africa. Most economists (including me) regarded the anti-globalization campaign as well-meaning but misguided, in opposing economic forces that were benefiting many developing countries—especially India and China—even though a stubborn minority of poor countries were unable to participate in the international flows of finance and trade because of their internal conflicts or dire political leadership. The mainstream view was that globalization, including the growing cross-border investment, was a force for good. One of the prime pieces of evidence was the large fall in poverty in India and especially China as they increasingly engaged in the global market. Despite the crisis, this remains true, and other countries have joined the ranks of so-called emerging markets, such as Indonesia, Nigeria, Ghana, and Mozambique.

Still, the continuing expansion of GDP in the developed world during the mid-2000s, as well as astoundingly rapid growth in the BRIC economies (Brazil, Russia, India, and China) and, to a lesser extent, in other emerging markets, fed the arrogance of the financial markets. There was said to be a "New Paradigm" of economic growth thanks to technology-driven increases in productivity. This was the era of books with titles like *Dow 36,000* and what Alan Greenspan famously described as "irrational exuberance."[1] Some economists warned early that the bubble would end disastrously.[2] Many more found it easier to assume that the buoyancy of financial markets would be sustained than to stick their necks out and predict economic cataclysm—it takes courage to stand out from the pack and make an extreme and unwelcome pronouncement. Besides, they had plentiful evidence that the U.S. Federal Reserve would make things right even if the markets did start to tumble, because that had happened repeatedly since 1987 during Mr. Greenspan's tenure as chairman. Monetary policy could be relied on to stimulate the economy, and the stock market if it weakened. After all, the Fed chairman was one of the most prominent believers in the New Paradigm.

It is widely known now, as it was not before 2008, that the financial markets were characterized not just by irrational exuberance but also by widespread fraud, deception (including self-deception), and market manipulation. Not to mention in the financial and corporate worlds alike a loss of ethical moorings, resulting in distasteful manifestations of greed. Even now, most members of the financial and business elite do not seem to have appreciated the extent to which they entered a separate moral universe; many seem to feel aggrieved, perceiving themselves to be unfairly scapegoated when it comes to assigning blame for the financial and economic crisis. This, too, is part of the arrogance, this belief that there were a few bad apples but nothing systemic had gone wrong in the way the financial industry and big businesses were being run.

So, in a classic tragedy, arrogance leads to folly. The follies have been many. The payment of multimillion-dollar and -pound remuneration packages by the elite to itself (all remuneration committees being filled with the same kind of people). The creation of toxic financial instruments that multiplied and focused risks. The self-delusions and inadequacies of regulatory bodies that grew too close to those people and businesses they were supposed to be regulating. Above all, the loss of perspective about the *purpose* of business, which is not at all the maximization of short-term profit or even shareholder value, but rather delivering goods and services to customers (in ways they might not even know they want), in a mutually beneficial transaction. Profit and share price increases are a side effect, not a goal.[3]

Finally, the tragic downfall, the nemesis. By the mid-2000s, despite the turmoil of the earlier Asian financial crisis and dot-com bust (in 2001), so-called Anglo-Saxon capitalism appeared triumphant. Its dominance was trumpeted by popular authors such as Thomas Friedman in his books *The*

Lexus and the Olive Tree and *The World Is Flat*. The message was: this is an uncomfortable ride but deal with it because global capitalism is sweeping the whole world before it. Yet some doubts started to emerge even before the onset of the financial crisis in late 2007.

There was, for example, not just the rise of the BRICs, but the prospect of their overtaking the West. The economist Jim O'Neill of Goldman Sachs coined the BRIC acronym. In 2001 he first published a report noting the rapid growth of these large emerging economies and their potential to overtake some of the leading developed economies in terms of the size of GDP. Maddison's historical data on GDP over the centuries showed that GDP per capita in China had been similar to that of the leading economies of the time, Britain, France, and the Netherlands, in 1800. Indeed, some economic historians have argued that China was the wealthier country until the start of the Industrial Revolution.[4] China subsequently stagnated, however, while the West grew rapidly and quickly pulled ahead. The years of communism were an economic as well as a human disaster for China, and GDP per capita declined after World War II. By about 1970 the typical inhabitant was no better off than his or her counterpart in the year 1000, according to Maddison's figures. The economic liberalization started tentatively by Deng Xiao Ping in 1981 triggered a growth snowball, however. Although per capita GDP in China remains well below Western levels, the country's total GDP either already has or soon will exceed that of the United States.[5] At the current annual growth rate, a little over 9 percent annually in recent years, China's GDP is doubling about once every eight years.

This pace of growth is unlikely to be sustained. Not only does the easy part of catching up occur first, but China also has significant demographic and social challenges, with a rapidly aging population and excess of men due to the one-child policy, little provision of welfare and pensions at present, and possibly a period of political turbulence. It also has a debt overhang due to a real estate bubble. Even so, China has without a doubt arrived on the global stage as both a political and an economic force. China's economic success has come about in large part through its integration into the flows of world trade and investment, its exports to the West and its overseas investments. Very many of the products businesses and consumers in the West buy are made or assembled in China, or have components made there. Global logistics chains have China's major ports as key links. For all that people in the West worry about losing jobs to China and other East Asian countries, it would be a massive economic wrench to unpick the way production has been reshaped across the globe in many industries. Simply, we depend on China for a large proportion of the manufactured products we buy. America's dependence appears even greater, since China holds more than one trillion dollars' worth of U.S. Treasury bonds, financing the U.S. government deficit, although that is in reality a mutually dysfunctional relationship.

This is quite a turnaround from the period of Western triumphalism. In China, the global financial crisis is termed the "North Atlantic crisis." From 2008 to 2012, real GDP in the OECD economies has grown by an average 0.9 percent a year, whereas in China it has been just over 9 percent a year. For all the uncertainties about China's future path, the financial crisis has had not only economic consequences but also lasting geopolitical effects.

In this chapter I will look at two fundamental issues the crisis raises about measuring economic output. The first is the obvious question about the role of the financial sector. For many years up to 2008, and even since then, politicians have praised the substantial contribution of financial services to the economy. Nonetheless, given the devastation they have caused in terms of unemployment, bankruptcies, and demands on the taxpayer, we have to ask how that devastation can be reconciled with the importance of finance in the GDP figures. The second issue is the deeper reevaluation of economic growth caused by a massive crisis in the market economy, and the economic theory on which policy has been based for the past generation. Have we been aiming at the wrong target all these years? The final chapter, looking at the future of GDP, will take up the questions raised here.

Value Added and Value Subtracted

The financial crisis has raised some profound questions about what finance is for and specifically how it is counted in GDP. Lifting the veil on its activities, ranging from foolhardy to fraudulent, has made it hard to understand how the financial sector has made a positive contribution to the economy at all. It has been the received wisdom for decades in the United States and the United Kingdom, with their large financial services sectors, that finance makes a significant contribution to GDP, to employment, to tax revenues, and to the balance of payments. Yet the provision of billions of pounds of direct taxpayer support to prevent banks from collapsing, and billions more in subsidized funding from central banks, certainly raised a question mark about this fiscal and economic contribution. The estimated cost of the crisis, including economic output forgone because of the resulting recession, is between one and five times the whole world's annual GDP.[6] "The scars from the current crisis seem likely to be felt for a generation," said Andrew Haldane, an executive director of the Bank of England.[7]

So, is finance being properly accounted for in the economic statistics? No.

A reason to be suspicious can be found in the United Kingdom's GDP statistics for the final quarter of 2008, the period during which Lehman Brothers went bankrupt and the global money markets were on the verge of ceasing to function. In that quarter, the statistics showed the fastest growth in the United Kingdom's financial sector on record. The figures suggested finance was making roughly the same contribution as manufacturing to the economy. Financial corporations' "gross operating surplus"[8] increased by 5.0 billion pounds to 20 billion pounds, and the financial sector's recorded share of the whole economy rose to 9 percent, and up again to 10.4 percent in 2009 (when manufacturing amounted to 11 percent), with the state propping up the sector through subsidized funding and direct state ownership. This is absurd. What on earth was going on with the statistics?

Measuring the financial sector is a well-known difficult problem in the national accounts. In the United Kingdom's national accounts, the financial sector appears to have grown twice as fast as the economy as a whole since 1850. Most of its growth has been concentrated in two periods, the episodes of globalization between the late nineteenth century and World War I and between the 1970s and 2007. Real GDP doubled between 1980 and 2008, but the measured real value added of the financial sector trebled. Similar trends are evident in the United States (where the share of the financial sector in total GDP rose from 2 percent in the 1950s to 8 percent in 2008) and in Europe. This was, in Andrew Haldane's phrase, more mirage than miracle.

The reason is the way financial output is measured. Most services charge customers a fee, and the fee revenues give statisticians the handle they need to measure output. Relatively few financial services involve direct fees or commissions. For the most part, banks do not generally sell services for a fee. A large proportion of their profits comes instead from the gap between the interest rates at which they can borrow (or pay depositors) and lend, or from trading activity. As the OECD GDP statistics manual puts it: "Measurement using the general formula [for constructing GDP] would result in their value added being very small, if not negative; in other words, their intermediate consumption would be greater than their sales!"[9]

Unable to imagine when this was written that banking could be subtracting value from the economy, statisticians sought to find a way of measuring these earnings from financial intermediation. So for many years the convention was to count financial services as the negative output of an imaginary segment of the economy. It is, to use a phrase from *Alice in Wonderland*, curiouser and curiouser. As the financial services industry grew throughout the 1980s, the approach changed again, and the 1993 update of the UN System of National Accounts introduced the concept of "financial intermediation services indirectly measured," or FISIM. This current measure compares banks' borrowing and lending rates on their loan and deposit portfolios to a risk-free "reference rate" such as the central bank's policy rate, and multiplies the difference by the stock of outstanding balances in each case. The practical difficulties are enormous, especially when it comes to translating this into an inflation-adjusted or real-terms figure.[10] But in principle it made sense as a way of measuring the service provided by banks in taking on risk.

One consequence, however, is that increased risk-taking is recorded as increased real growth in financial services. So do very low official 'reference rates,' as we have had since the crisis. As Andrew Haldane and his coauthors put it, what's so special about banks taking risks? "[It] is not clear that bearing risk is, in itself, a productive activity. Any household or corporate investing in a risky debt security also bears credit and liquidity risk. The act of investing capital in a risky asset is a fundamental feature of capital markets and is not specific to the activities of banks. Conceptually, therefore, it is not clear that risk-based income flows should represent bank output."[11] Taking risks is not a valuable service to the rest of the economy, although managing risk is. Haldane goes on to note that banks' reported profits have been flattered in the same way by ignoring the statistical effect of the banks simply taking greater risks by leveraging their equity. The profits were "illusory," although of course the bonuses were not. Similarly, the finance sector's contribution still reflects the very low levels of reference interest rates, rather than a positive service to society, by lending for productive real investment, for example.

The FISIM statistical mirage affects all countries' GDP. One study of the United States concludes: "Making conservative assumptions, we show that the current official method overestimates the service output of the commercial banking industry by at least 21% (amounting to $116.8 billion in 2007:Q4 for example) and GDP by 0.3% ($52.9 billion in 2007:Q4 for example) between 1997 and 2007."[12] For the Eurozone, adjusting for banks' risk-taking would reduce the measured output of the financial sector by 25–40 percent. If the same factor were applied in the United Kingdom, the measured contribution of the financial sector would have been 6–7.5 percent of GDP in 2008, rather than 9 percent.[13] These figures are staggering: the size of the financial sector in recent years has been overstated by at least one-fifth, maybe even by as much as one-half.

Why does it matter that the contribution of the financial services industry to GDP is overstated? The answer is that political leaders shape economic policy around key sectors. During the financial crisis, the industry's lobbying has had a substantial impact on political decisions about regulatory reform, not just because investment banks make donations to political parties, but also because politicians genuinely believe the industry to be fundamentally important to jobs and economic growth.[14] "Our economy needs the industry," wrote Alastair Darling, the U.K. chancellor of the exchequer, in his memoir of the crisis, despite having experienced the height of the crisis when the industry had, on the contrary, nearly torpedoed the economy.[15] The former U.S. Federal Reserve chairman Alan Greenspan explicitly linked increased prosperity as measured by GDP to a large and complex finance sector: "During the postwar years, the degree of financial complexity has appeared to grow with the rising division of labour, globalisation, and the level of technology. One measure of that complexity, the share of gross domestic product devoted to finance and insurance, has increased dramatically. In America for example, it rose from 2.4 per cent in 1947 to 7.4 per cent in 2008, and to a still larger 7.9 per cent during the severe contraction of 2009."[16]

This view that finance is a strategically important sector of the economy developed alongside the changes in statistical methodology. The original SNA (in 1953) had shown the financial services industry as making either a negative or a small positive contribution to GDP. Finance was a more or less "unproductive" activity because the interest flows (now measured by the FISIM construct) were broadly treated as an intermediate input of the finance sector and therefore netted out of the sector's final value-added contribution to GDP. In the United States from 1947 to 1993, the net interest revenue from financial intermediation (labeled the imputed bank service charge, IBSC) was counted as an input to other sectors of the economy. This approach was formalized worldwide in the revised 1968 SNA, when the IBSC was "considered wholly intermediate consumption and, more pointedly, as the input/ expense exclusively of a notional industry sector with no output of its own. That is correct: an imaginary industry supplying no products or services was theorized into being as the 'buyer' of banks' intermediation. The 'services' of financial intermediaries were still deemed productive outputs, therefore, yet rather than being traceable to other, tangible sectors of the national economy, they now disappeared into what was effectively the black hole of a dummy industry with a negative value-added equal (but opposite in sign) to the IBSC."[17] The United Kingdom adopted this approach in 1973, France in 1975. This change started to turn finance from a conceptually unproductive into a productive sector. The 1993 SNA accelerated the reenvisioning of finance. In a study of international banking, Brett Christophers writes: "Instead of assessing banks' borrowing and lending activities together, and intimating that the combination constituted a portfolio of services whose collective value could be imputed by deducting interest paid on the former from interest generated by the latter, SNA 1993 separates the two functions and defines each— independently—as a productive activity whose output can be measured."[18] Ironically, the United Kingdom's Office for National Statistics implemented this treatment of FISIM fully for the first time in the 2008 figures.[19] This is an important conceptual change. It portrays finance as an economic activity like any other—just as a manufacturer takes raw materials and transforms them into more valuable products, banks take a risk-free return and transform it into a higher return by taking risks, providing a service to both the source of the funds—the ultimate depositor or lender—and the recipient or borrower. But the absurdity of recording big increases in the contribution made by financial services to GDP as the biggest financial crisis in a generation or two got under way indicates that the statistical approach is mistaken. Economists have begun to suggest methods for adjusting the FISIM figure to take account of risk-taking behavior by banks. No doubt other technical suggestions will come along.

There is, however, an underlying question about whether finance should be included in GDP at all, and what we mean by "productive" behavior. The final part of this chapter raises some questions about "productivity" and, more fundamentally, what it is we value in the economy. The financial crisis has led many people to question the way only the monetary values that are measured by GDP seem to matter. The financial sector seems to symbolize the undue weight society gives to the growth of some activities rather than others. The crisis has given fresh impetus to the continuing debate about whether we should be measuring GDP and paid-for output, or instead looking for a measure of well-being or social welfare.

THE PRODUCTION BOUNDARY

Adam Smith, as we saw in chapter 1, considered all services to be "unproductive," and that certainly included banking. In his book on the role of finance in the economy, Brett Christophers writes, "The real problem lies not so much with particular measures of productiveness but with our underlying social fixation with identifying the economically productive and distinguishing it from the unproductive."[20] In principle, GDP avoids the need to distinguish productive from unproductive because it measures what people pay for, and their willingness to pay can be taken as an indicator of productive value (although of course there might be alternatives to money as a measure of value). Yet, as we've seen in the case of financial services, and also in the case of public services paid for via taxation, this leaves some practical difficulties when statisticians or politicians want to include in the definition of "the economy" activities that people do not pay for directly. The economists of the eighteenth and nineteenth centuries were not troubled by leaving government spending and banking out of their definition of national income, whereas subsequently the economic consensus has favored including them.

Richard Stone, one of the founding fathers of national accounts, was perfectly up-front about the arbitrariness of what was included and how: "This treatment, whereby commercial products are valued at market price, government services are valued at cost and unpaid household activities are simply ignored, is not a matter of principle but of practical convenience. It can be defended, therefore, only on practical grounds."[21]

The imaginary line dividing productive from unproductive activity is called the "production boundary." There is no sharp division in reality, so at the boundary there are arbitrary decisions, and this can be simply a matter of convenience. The border also becomes self-fulfilling, though, as being included in the national accounts definition of GDP is taken as a mark of "productiveness." As Christophers explains, "Because they provide measures of economic output, and especially because they enable different industries' or sectors' relative contributions to output to be quantified—'this sector represents half of our national economy, that sector only a quarter,' and so forth—the national accounts have come to represent a perfect vehicle for the ongoing enactment of our obsession."[22]

There have been several different kinds of debate over the years about the production boundary. One concerns the role of the "informal" or "shadow" or "underground" economy (I'm going to stick with the label *informal*). By definition, there are no reliable official statistics on economic activity operating outside of the tax net and the law. Shading into this is the issue of what statisticians call "household production," or unpaid work inside the family. The well-known paradox is that a widower who marries his former housekeeper is reducing GDP since he is no longer paying her a wage. Another debate asks whether activities that do not contribute positively to welfare (not so much banking as, say, legal services, arms sales, polluting industries, and the like) should be excluded from the measure of output, GDP. Advocates of these kinds of adjusted measures also tend to be keen on measuring people's well-being or happiness directly through surveys. A related argument is that the rich countries of the West do not need any more economic growth. This "no growth" advocacy is linked to concern about the environment, both in recent years and a generation ago.[23] Let's take these in turn.

THE INFORMAL ECONOMY

In 1987, Italy announced an overnight increase in its level of GDP. Its official statisticians decided to start including an estimate of the unofficial economy in their figures. It increased the size of the economy by about a fifth, taking Italy past the United Kingdom to become the fifth biggest in the world, just behind France at number four. It was labeled *il sorpasso*, the overtaking. "A wave of euphoria swept over Italians after economists recalibrated their statistics, taking into account for the first time the country's formidable underground economy of tax evaders and illegal workers," reported the *New York Times*.[24]

The observation and labeling of the informal economy originated with the anthropologist Keith Hart, based on his fieldwork in Ghana in the late 1960s and early 1970s. Subsequently, the extensiveness of informal economic activity has been widely recognized. It means business carried out without paying taxes or acquiring permits or observing all government regulations such as health and safety or employment laws. There are pluses and minuses. The informal economy is highly entrepreneurial and creates lots of jobs. In some countries it occurs either because government regulations are onerous—such as high import duties on manufactured goods shipped into developing countries, or finicky rules about the placement of shelves or sinks in developed countries—or because people are so poor they need to earn money however they can.

Some off-the-books activity occurs everywhere, and its scale can be estimated in various ways, for instance using indicators such as electricity consumption or the use of cash. The estimates include both outright criminal activities including organized crime, and illegal or unreported but largely benign businesses. In developing countries, the proportion of GDP accounted for by economic activity that stays outside the official net for taxes and scrutiny is high: the "informal" economy will be large in a poor country where many people work as self-employed entrepreneurs, farmers, or day laborers. In developed countries, the proportion is variable, ranging from around 7 percent of GDP in the United States and 8 percent of GDP in Switzerland to 20 percent in Italy and 25 percent in Greece (all 2012 estimates). The average is about 15 percent of GDP. In the formerly communist "transition" economies, the typical share of the shadow economy is 21–30 percent, and in poorer developing economies 35–44 percent of GDP. The informal economy has been growing in size around the world. Friedrich Schneider writes, "Studies based on data for several countries suggest that the major driving forces behind the size and growth of the shadow economy are an increasing burden of tax and social security payments, combined with rising restrictions in the official labor market."[25]

After a bit of controversy about Italy's decision to adjust GDP for the unofficial economy, the fuss that time died down quickly. However, Italy made a similar revision a second time around in 2014, this time including additional illegal activities—specifically prostitution and the drugs business. It was not alone in doing so. Most EU countries made the same change during 2014, in order to comply with new standards set by Eurostat, the EU's statistical agency, reflecting the latest internationally agreed definitions. The new methodology—which involved other changes too—added about 4% to the UK's level of GDP, 2.5% to Spain's, probably more in the case of Finland and Sweden. In truth, the measurement of sex and drugs accounts for a small part of the new changes, but it does catch the imagination. For example, the official statisticians at the UK's ONS have picked six drugs—crack cocaine, powder cocaine, heroin, cannabis, ecstasy, and amphetamines—and will use crime surveys to estimate the number of users of each drug, estimate annual use per person, and apply street prices. They will use the police's estimates of on-street prostitution, and calculate future changes by using the changes in the male population. They will link prices to the price of going into a lap-dancing club. It is more than a little surreal to imagine the serious statisticians implementing these particular methodological changes.

Although hard to measure, the largely cash-based informal economy of moonlighting, avoiding taxes and regulations, and engaging in illegal activities, but thereby creating work and output, has been placed inside the production boundary. It involves monetary transactions in the market economy, so this is all perfectly logical, if somewhat bizarre.

For there is other informal economic activity that isn't included, largely because no money changes hands. It's what economists call "own-production" or "household production." This means all the work done within the family for its own use: the cooking, cleaning, child care, vegetable growing, sewing, carpentry, and so on. All of this can be bought, outsourced outside the household; but much is not. The main reason given for not counting unpaid housework as part of "the economy," while paid housework (or prostitution for that matter) is counted, is the difficulty of measuring it. Well, *difficulty* is surely not the right word. It can be measured by surveys, like many other economic statistics, but generally official statistical agencies have never bothered—perhaps because it has been carried out mainly by women and seen as unimportant.

From time to time, a few countries have conducted "time-use surveys" to find out how much household production takes place, and valued its contribution to the economy by applying the wage rates that prevail for each kind of work if it has to be paid for. The United States has continuous time-use surveys now; Australia and Canada conduct them reasonably frequently, as do a number of other countries. But many do not; the United Kingdom last carried out a large survey in

2000–2001. Its Office for National Statistics is to start publishing regular estimates of unpaid household work for the first time from mid-2015, based on alternative approaches—for example, taking the number of households with washing machines, estimating a number of loads per week, and using the price of going to the launderette to calculate a value. Preliminary estimates suggest unpaid childcare is worth about three times as much as financial services, while household laundering is worth about four-fifths of financial services' contribution to the economy.[26] There are long-term trends, such as the move by many women into paid work since the 1960s, and an increase in leisure time in many of the rich countries. There are also some changes over the business cycle, as people economize on paying for services such as cleaners or eating out when there is a recession. (The picture in poor countries is different because subsistence farming is common in many cases, so the unpaid informal economy will be consistently important.) Even in good times, however, the scale of this informal, unpaid work is significant: it accounts for more than half of all the time people spend working. If this is valued at money wages paid for similar work, it is equivalent to 1.85 times the size of the conventional national product figure for the United Kingdom in 2001.[27] Although the figure will vary among countries, the importance of this activity, conventionally but arbitrarily excluded from official GDP statistics, is universal. It would be paradoxical if most statistical agencies continue not to produce estimates of household production, if they are now going to follow the official methodology and try to measure illegal marketed activities.

Economic Output and Welfare

The question of whether to include activities at home such as cooking and child care takes us into the question about the extent to which we want to measure well-being, or "social welfare" in the technical jargon of economics, rather than simply output. The time spent on "home production" has increased over the decades, while paid work hours have declined. Yet, although child care and cooking are certainly work, they bring pleasure too, and some people have argued that the increase in time spent on them is actually leisure rather than work, and so not really part of the economy. I think this is a red herring, because a lot of people enjoy their paid work, or some of it, as well. Should that be deducted from GDP because it's enjoyable? Obviously not. Interestingly, this definitional question has cropped up in live politics. For example, Laura Perrins, a British lawyer who left her job to look after her young children at home called in to a radio show to criticize Nick Clegg, then deputy prime minister, over a new coalition government tax credit to help mothers working outside the home pay for child care. "I'm just wondering why the coalition is discriminating against mothers like me who care for their children at home.... I just feel that this provision is to bump up the GDP numbers, because if I was to look after somebody else's children that would count as a GDP number, which is all that I think the Treasury care about."[28]

There is a real issue here. Should we be aiming for a measure of enjoyment, or happiness, or well-being, instead of GDP? This is a vigorous debate at present. One of the consequences of the financial crisis has been to raise widespread doubts about the merits of markets, and economics in general. To the chagrin of many economists, who do not recognize their own work in the attacks made on the subject, economics gets the blame for the intellectual climate of advocacy for markets that made the financial excesses possible and, more broadly, seems to have made short-term profit the arbiter of most areas of life. Michael Sandel says we must "call into question an assumption that informs much market-oriented thinking. This is the assumption that all goods are commensurable, that all goods can be translated without loss into a single measure or unit of value."[29] So a campaign to promote "happiness" rather than economic growth has gathered momentum.

The anti-GDP campaign has its roots in a famous article by the economist Richard Easterlin. He recorded an apparent paradox. Looking at the evidence at a single point in time, people are happier in richer countries than in poorer ones (we are talking about averages); but looking at one country over time, rising GDP per capita does not translate into increased happiness. As a number of economists have noted, the paradox is due to the nature of the statistics: GDP is an artificial figure that can increase without limit, whereas happiness (reported by people in surveys or diaries) has an upper limit. The relationship between the two is like that between GDP and, say, height, or life expectancy—they are linked, just not proportionately over time.[30] The silliness of the notion that rising GDP does not increase happiness at all is even easier to see when you remember that a recession, when GDP declines just a little, makes people very unhappy. What's more, given that productivity increases over time, GDP has to rise to keep unemployment from going up; and higher unemployment would also make people unhappy.

So the apparently obvious conclusion is based on a misunderstanding of the kinds of statistics being used to relate happiness and GDP. "Happiness" is measured from surveys, with respondents asked to rate their feelings on a scale of 1 to

3 or 1 to 10. It can never climb above the top of the scale, even with centuries of data. GDP is a constructed statistic that can rise without limit. If you plot a line that climbs extremely gently over time against a line that rises steadily by 2–3 percent a year, they will look unrelated even if they are not. It turns out from a number of more recent studies that reported happiness is strongly positively linked with the change or growth in GDP per capita from year to year.

There is a valid point that economic growth measured by GDP over time is not an accurate indicator of well-being or social welfare. (I'm going to use the term *social welfare*, but bear in mind that it does not mean welfare payments.) In the children's book *The Lion, the Witch and the Wardrobe*, the White Witch uses enchanted Turkish Delight candy to ensnare Edmund. Once he has had one piece, he cannot resist more. Consumerism is an addiction too. Psychology offers insights into the rat race and consumerism. The experimental evidence is that most people care more about status and therefore their relative income than they do about the absolute level of income. The "conspicuous consumption" first named by Thorstein Veblen is a kind of arms race of status, and one that the excesses of corporate pay have let rip in the past quarter century. What's more, the satisfaction we get from extra income and purchases wears off quickly, leaving us, like Edmund in the story, hungry for another fix. The evocative technical term for this is the *hedonic treadmill*.

If money is an addiction, it's not surprising that some people think society needs help being weaned off it. Economists such as Robert Frank and Richard Layard advocate a tax on purchases of luxury items. Another policy recommendation has had more traction: that instead of measuring GDP we should be measuring happiness. In the United Kingdom there is even a Campaign for Happiness. The government leapt on its bandwagon, ordering the Office for National Statistics to start a survey to measure happiness levels around the country.[31] Grotesquely, there are cheerleaders for the king of Bhutan because of his claim that he seeks to increase gross national happiness, when Bhutan is one of the poorest and one of the more authoritarian countries in the world.

The fashion for measuring happiness is based on two approaches to the evidence. One kind is the approach using top-down aggregate economic data that Richard Easterlin used in his original paper. Other studies look at the statistical links between the level of happiness people report in surveys and their personal circumstances: are they married? Employed? In good health? The results are comfortingly sensible. People are happier if they are in a job, married, healthy, or have a religious faith. People like spending time with their friends and family but not their boss, and hate commuting. There is a life cycle of happiness: in general, we are least happy in middle age ("middle age" ranging from thirty-six in the United Kingdom to sixty-six in Portugal).[32] Women tend to be happier than men, although that relative advantage may have diminished over the decades. It is not clear, however, that there are all that many policy implications in these results. We already knew that voters hate it when unemployment goes up. The government can hardly start mandating marriage and churchgoing to enforce greater happiness. The most important new practical finding from these studies is that mental ill-health is a major contributor to unhappiness, and yet almost everywhere it is a low priority in public health policies.

Still, no matter that the empirical evidence for the happiness bandwagon is weak. The idea that once countries had grown comfortably rich, it is folly to pursue further economic growth, has struck a chord. It is important, though, to be clear that GDP is not and was not intended to be a measure of national welfare. Economists have repeatedly cautioned themselves and others not to get the two mixed up. For example, Moses Abramowitz, a noted expert on business cycles and economic growth, said in 1959: "We must be highly skeptical of the view that long-term changes in the rate of growth of welfare can be gauged even roughly from changes in the rate of growth of output." Yet despite such cautions, economists and politicians often talk as if GDP and welfare are more or less the same. What policymakers should be aiming for is welfare or well-being, not more GDP for its own sake. "Economists all know that, and yet their everyday use of GNP as the standard measure of economic performance apparently conveys the impression that they are evangelistic worshippers of GNP," remark William Nordhaus and James Tobin.[33]

Besides, whether or not the task *ought* to be measuring welfare rather than GDP was debated in the early years of GDP's development, as we saw in chapter 1, and it has been debated ever since. Remember that Simon Kuznets, working on measuring national income in the 1930s, wanted to deduct spending on harmful items or activities such as armaments, advertising, and financial speculation—along with outlays that he described as 'necessary evils' (such as "subways and expensive housing") to enable other activity to take place. He added, "Obviously the removal of such items from national income estimates, difficult as it would be, would make national income totals much better gauges of the volume of services produced, for comparison among years and among nations."[34]

In fact, there have been numerous initiatives over the years to develop an index of welfare as opposed to GDP, which measures output only. One widely used by economists, especially in discussing developing countries, is the Human Development Index, described in chapter 3. The structure of the index puts the Scandinavian economies at or near the top, instead of the United States, and some middle-income countries such as India lower in the ranking than their GDP per capita figures alone would indicate, because of extensive poverty and poor health. The HDI was first published in 1990, and has been widely adopted by economists as a useful single indicator of national welfare.

Many other alternatives have often been driven by environmental concerns, and specifically address the point that things that are bad for the environment in one way or another are good for GDP. For example, spending on pollution-abatement equipment adds to GDP, as does investment in the extraction of oil or natural gas. GDP does not account for the negative effect of pollution or the depletion of natural assets.

One prominent example of an index that tried to address these problems was the Measure of Economic Welfare (MEW) proposed in 1972 by William Nordhaus and James Tobin, in response to the intellectual challenge posed by the environmentalist Paul Ehrlich. They adjusted GNP (working from that rather than GDP) in three ways: classifying all spending as consumption, investment, or intermediate; taking account of the value of leisure and of household work, and the benefits of investment by consumers in capital goods; and correcting for what they called "the disamenities of urbanization."[35] Their calculations showed that the MEW had increased somewhat less rapidly than GNP in the United States during the postwar years. Their conclusion, though, was that GNP was good enough: "Is growth obsolete? We think not. Although GNP and other national income aggregates are imperfect measures of welfare, the broad picture of secular progress which they convey remains after correction of their most obvious deficiencies."

That conclusion did not win over environmentalists, and efforts continued to develop other alternatives. One of the best-known is the Index of Sustainable Economic Welfare (ISEW), launched in 1989 by Herman Daly and John Cobb. It evolved into the Genuine Progress Indicator (GPI) in the 1990s. Both start from consumption spending as measured for the GDP statistics, add some household production, and make a series of deductions for items like defense spending, the costs of crime and environmental degradation, and resource use. These indexes, which have been applied in a number of countries including the United States and the United Kingdom, are defined in such a way that they will almost always grow more slowly than real GDP. You can try this for yourself on websites that allow you to create a personal ISEW, giving different components weights according to your personal priorities; I could not make the index match GDP growth no matter what weights I tried.[36] Besides, although it is useful for everyone to be able to create their own policy target, depending on how much they care about crime rather than clean rivers, so they know for whom to vote in the next election, the published official statistics need to be impersonal, not personalized.

The alternative indicators also err in only subtracting from measured GDP. In addition to adding in the value of household production, they ought to be adjusting the measure upward to take account of the improvements that come from innovation. These are difficult indeed to measure. How could one begin to estimate the impact on society's welfare of new products such as antibiotics in the 1940s, or central heating and air conditioning, or the Internet and mobile phones? Earlier, we saw how hard it is to capture quality improvements in some items in GDP. In chapter 6 I'll return to the challenge of measuring innovation and the variety of products and services available. For now, it's enough to acknowledge that, as the economic historian Brad DeLong expresses it, "Modern growth is so fast it's off the scale."[37]

Although GDP does not measure welfare directly, it does contribute to it and is highly correlated with things that definitely do affect our well-being, such as life expectancy and infant mortality. Some relatively tightly defined adjustments would give a measure significantly closer to welfare than the present definition of GDP. The economist Martin Weitzman proposed using Net National Product (NNP), which he showed was the yield generated by the economy's stock of capital, and therefore indicated the maximum sustainable rate of consumption. If it is less than actual consumption, then society has been living beyond its means by using up capital. Nicholas Oulton, an advocate of improving GDP rather than ditching it, recommends some other changes. The most important is including environmental capital: "For example, the UK national accounts include mineral oil exploration as part of gross investment but depletion of oil and gas stocks by extraction is not included in depreciation and so NNP is overstated," Oulton says.[38] On the other hand, he notes that conventional national accounts omit the way innovation and productivity gains will increase the amount that can be sustainably consumed from a given amount of capital (financial, physical, and natural) assets. This is a question of growing concern, and something the future approach to measuring the economy needs to take on board.

Meanwhile, one alternative approach to measuring the economy's progress has had some influence, and that is the idea of a "dashboard" of indicators. France's former president

Nicolas Sarkozy asked two Nobel Memorial Prize–winning economists, Joseph Stiglitz and Amartya Sen, to join the French economist Jean-Paul Fitoussi in a thorough assessment of economic statistics. Their commission worked carefully through all the arguments for developing an alternative to GDP, summed up in this section. They concluded that a better approach, rather than trying to combine different kinds of figures together in one indicator, would be to collect and publish statistics on a range of indicators we can be confident contribute to social welfare.[39] Some countries' statistical agencies have already adopted this dashboard approach. I liked the Australian example, which for a while was published annually as "Measuring Australia's Progress," because citizens are consulted on what measures they want included. But there are others. One of the most sophisticated dashboard at present is the OECD's Better Life Index (http://www.oecdbetterlifeindex.org/), which is a visualization of countries' relative rankings depending on eleven components, ranging from income to work-life balance, housing to the environment. The weights are easy to change and it is straightforward to compare how different countries fare depending on which component is given greater weight. Another example is the Economic Well-being publication the UK's Office for National Statistics published for the first time at the end of 2014, to be published regularly alongside the standard GDP figures. It consists of existing economic statistics presented in ways that are informative about living standards, the distribution of income, changes in wealth as well as income, and so on. Statistics New Zealand publishes a similar set of 'Progress Indicators' on its website, allowing users to select economic, social, and environmental perspectives.

The Better Life Index and the Economic Well-Being statistics are not tools that could be used for macroeconomic policy, but they present the trade-offs between different outcomes in a very accessible way. This is an important step in enabling a public debate about economic policy that is not wholly geared toward short-term growth, but takes into account sustainability too. These innovations reflect statisticians responding to both the academic debate about how to track the many dimensions of economic and social change and a growing popular demand to go 'beyond GDP.' Unfortunately, though, there is no evidence yet of dashboards displacing the prime status of GDP growth in political debate.

SIX

The Future: Twenty-first-Century GDP

This book has described the origins and evolution of GDP, the measure of economic performance used all the time in the media and in the world of economic policy. GDP is a relatively modern way of measuring the size of economic output, and as we saw differs from earlier methods. For example, early definitions of "national income" did not include government spending, because governments before the late nineteenth and early twentieth century had such limited functions. Paying for war, or for the justice system, was seen as a necessary evil reducing national income, rather than a positive contribution to the economy.

Although paying for World War II was the trigger for the modern definition of GDP, after the 1930s the government also began to undertake more collective consumption and investment, spending our tax money on our joint behalf either on services and transfers, or on building roads and other infrastructure. The experience of the Great Depression had already naturally focused political attention on how fast—or not—economic output was growing, and governments wanted both to measure and to influence it. The collection of statistics in the shape of GDP and the national accounts went hand in hand with the development of macroeconomic policy, the attempt by governments to influence growth using the tools of taxation, government spending, money, and interest rates.

The construction of GDP, along with the collection of the necessary raw statistics to do so, were not straightforward activities, even in those early days when the economy was less complex than it is now. It took decades for national accounts to be created for more than a handful of countries, and for economists and statisticians to create and refine the methods for comparing GDP over time and across countries. Adjusting GDP in dollar or nominal terms for inflation to give "real" GDP is one fundamental step. The constant improvements in the quality of products as well as the introduction of new goods and services over time have made it ever harder to calculate a meaningful general price level: today's laptop is a vastly different machine from one bought just a few years ago for the same price, and the price of computing was infinite a few decades ago because computers did not exist. It is hard to capture this transformation in a single price index. Converting from one currency into another is another complicated task, given how significantly economies differ from one another in their structure and what consumers spend their incomes on. So international comparisons of economic performance are difficult (not that this has stopped economists from making them); and it may well be that the impression we have of the growth of different economies at different times is simply wrong.

National accounts experts have also sought to enhance their work over the decades, responding to a range of challenges in addition to these. In particular, both growing environmental awareness and the seemingly slow progress in economic development measured by GDP per capita in many poor countries have prompted interest in alternative indicators. An old debate has been reopened, namely, whether or not a measure of welfare should replace GDP as the target for economic policy.

Economic crisis is another trigger for interest in alternative measurements. The combination of the Great Depression and World War II brought us GDP in the first place, replacing earlier notions about "the economy" and how to measure it. The crisis of the mid-1970s combined with the nascent environmental movement to prompt an initial wave of interest in new types of indicator, although these took a decade or so to come to fruition. The present crisis has breathed new life into a range of alternative approaches such as "happiness," welfare indexes, and dashboard approaches, not to mention raising a serious question mark over the current standard method for calculating the contribution financial services make to the economy.

Is this crisis the time for leaving behind GDP and turning to some new way of understanding and measuring "the economy"? In this final chapter, I conclude that we should not be in a rush to ditch GDP. Yet it is a measure of the economy best suited to an earlier era. "GDP is a statistic designed for mass production. It's a simple counting—the number of units made. It falls short in measuring intangible benefits.... Nobody ever said quantity was the spice of life," as the Dallas Fed has put it.[1] So I also want to look at three issues that suggest we might move toward a different approach in time. The character of the economy is changing, and the way we measure it will have to change too, although exactly what the new way we think about "the economy" might turn out to be is too big a question for this book.

Those three issues are:

• the complexity of the economy now, reflected in innovation, the pace of introduction of new products and
services, and also in globalization and the way goods
are made in complicated global production chains;

• the increasing share of advanced economies made up
of services and "intangibles," including online activities with no price, rather than physical products, which
makes it impossible to separate quality and quantity or
even think about quantities at all; and

• the urgency of questions of sustainability, requiring
more attention to be paid to the depletion of resources
and assets, which is undermining potential future GDP
growth.

COMPLEXITY

The United States in 1998 offered 185 TV channels, 141 over-
the-counter painkillers, and eighty-seven brands of soft drink.
These figures all represented big increases since 1970, when
there had been five TV channels, five painkillers, and twenty
types of soft drink. By 1998, there were 340 kinds of breakfast cereal, up from 160, and fifty brands of bottled water on
offer, compared with sixteen in 1970. The number of types
of personal computer had risen from zero to four hundred
in twenty-eight years, the number of websites from zero to
nearly five million.[2] Earlier, I referred to the increase in the
variety of products and services that make up GDP in all the
advanced economies; these specific comparisons just help
indicate how dramatic the proliferation of variety has been.
Indeed, variety could be considered one of the key indicators

of economic development. To be poor is to have little choice available, and the increase in possibility is the most important aspect of escaping from poverty. On this view, economic development is a combination of increasing individual capacities or skills to be able to take advantage of opportunities, and increasing the range of opportunities and choices available. Economic development is an increase in freedom. One aspect of this is the variety of goods and services available in the economy, from the trivial to the profoundly important.[3]

It is surprisingly hard, though, to find statistics on the number of different product types available. The Federal Reserve Bank of Dallas 1998 Annual Report, from which the figures here are taken, is one of the few estimates available even now. The main reason it is so difficult is simply that the statistics are not collected by official agencies. The surveys sent to businesses ask about volumes of output—number of pairs of shoes made by a shoe factory—and prices charged, but not number of styles. So official statistics are published as aggregate categories: "shoes." The fact that I can choose high-tech walking boots, or running shoes that will cushion my knees and ankles, or vegan shoes, or shoes shaped to exercise my thighs as I walk, or gorgeous red high heel shoes, or ugly but ultra-comfortable sandals, or sneakers I designed myself on the vendor's website—none of that features in the statistics.

Still, even if we haven't been counting it, it is obvious that variety is increasing in the case of consumer goods and services we experience every day. Increasingly, we can even customize what we buy, from shoes to (famously) Dell computers—customization being the ultimate in increased variety, every item different. There is even the promise of customized medicines for fighting cancer and other diseases, drugs tailored to each individual patient's genetic code. There is some evidence of both the increase in variety in specific examples (such as the number of book titles published, or the number of types of breakfast cereal), and of the resulting increases in consumer welfare.

Why does this affect GDP, though? Think about a place setting for a meal. My contribution to GDP is the same whether I manufacture a knife, fork, and spoon, or three spoons. GDP just counts the number of items.

GDP underrecords growth by failing to capture fully the increase in the range of products in the economy. It is a poor way to measure innovation and customization, and the extent to which it undermeasures them is extremely large. It also fails to record at all another increasingly important category, namely, preventive goods or services. Take driverless cars for example. One of these will increase GDP by the same amount as any other kind of car, or perhaps by more if statisticians calculate a hedonic price index to adjust for its improved quality—after all, the human can sit back and relax in a driverless car. But GDP will not capture at all the benefit of a reduction in the number of accidents as driverless cars spread, assuming they live up to the high hopes that this will be the result.

In chapter 5, I noted the distinction between GDP and welfare and yet the strong link between the two. The trend toward greater choice or even customization increases the wedge between the two concepts. "We might not see faster growth rates or surges in productivity, but mass customization will pay off for America. Resources are wasted guessing what customers want. When more products are customized, we won't squander money on clothing that sits in the closet because it doesn't fit or compact discs with only one or two songs we really like. And goods won't languish on dealers' shelves. Achieving a higher standard of living with fewer demands on natural and labor resources will help ease price pressures and continue this decade's good news on inflation," wrote the Dallas Fed's economists in 1998.[4] The promises of "mass customization" they dangled before their readers' eyes in 1998 are coming to pass, including TV shows on demand so viewers, not schedulers, determine the evening's viewing; or clothing made-to-measure for the midmarket many, not just the wealthy few.

Separate statistical headaches arise from the increasing complexity of the economy, due to the fact that most goods are now "made" in global supply chains. The components will be manufactured in a number of countries, shipped around the world to be assembled in one place, and shipped back out to their destination markets. This is true of goods as apparently simple as a shirt or as sophisticated as an iPhone.[5] China, of course, has been the main country of assembly in these global chains, but other Asian countries and their Latin American competitors Brazil and Mexico have been gaining ground.

Price indexes do not, however, capture the large price declines when outsourcing occurs, so import prices have been greatly overstated and import volumes underrecorded.[6] In addition, trade statistics do not net out the intermediate stages: the whole value of the iPhone imported from China to the United States counts toward the U.S. current account of the balance of payments. "The traditional method of recording trade has failed to reflect the actual value chain distribution and painted a distorted picture about the bilateral trade relations. The Sino-U.S. bilateral trade imbalance has been greatly inflated," according to one study of the statistics.[7] Value-added trade statistics are now becoming available, and their study is likely to change the big picture we hold in our minds about the shape of the world economy.

Productivity

If economists were to play a game of word association, the one that would leap to mind on hearing *productivity* would be *puzzle*. I already quoted Robert Solow's famous 1987 version of the productivity puzzle: "You can see the computer age everywhere but in the productivity figures." As discussed in chapter 5, the New Economy era from the mid-1990s to 2001 did see productivity growth increase in the official figures, although that has slowed down again in the postcrisis economy. But a different "puzzle" may have emerged in the United Kingdom: despite more or less zero GDP growth since 2008, employment has increased. By definition, this implies (at best) no increase in productivity.[8]

Why is productivity puzzling?

It is because of the second increasingly serious issue for GDP as a measure of the economy, namely, that the economy consists less and less of material items.[9] It is relatively straightforward to measure economic output when you can count the number of cars or refrigerators or nails or microwave meals being shipped from factories. But how do you measure the output of nurses, accountants, garden designers, musicians, software developers, health care assistants, and so on? The only way is to count how many of them there are and how many "customers" they provide with a service, but this entirely overlooks the *quality* of the service, which is of great importance.

Just as "output" is a concept best suited to an economy made up of products rather than services, and similar, mass-produced products at that, so is "productivity." The word is used in general terms to mean efficiency or effectiveness. The actual definition used by economist is the amount of output produced per unit of inputs. Inputs are labor, capital, land,

and material resources. Usually economists are talking about labor productivity because it is easy to measure the number of workers, and much harder to measure capital. So on this definition, productivity is the amount produced per worker, or GDP per person employed (or per person-hour worked, to be more precise).

This is fine for washing machines or cartons of breakfast cereal. But only a small part of GDP in countries such as the United States and the EU nations consists of physical products. For all of us who are office workers, it will be obvious that measuring our productivity is hard, but certainly isn't well captured by our organization's revenues, adjusted for our pay rises over time to give a real-terms measure, then divided by the number of employees—which is the GDP-based approach. The quality of what we do is an intrinsic part of our "output." Or take nurses: are they more productive if they see more patients per day, or spend more time with fewer patients? It depends on the exact character of their work that day (taking samples for blood tests, or caring for someone in intensive care?), and on the outcomes of their work (does the patient get better faster? or feel more cared for?). To give another example, conventional statistics would count a musician as more productive if she gave twice as many performances by performing a Mozart concerto at double speed.[10] The economist William Baumol identified this productivity challenge in the performing arts long ago, as well as its application to other services such as health care.

The same phenomenon applies in the increasingly creative digital economy. The tech guru Kevin Kelly writes:

> Nobody ever suggested that Picasso should spend fewer hours painting per picture in order to boost his wealth or improve the economy. The value he added to the economy could not be

optimized for productivity. Generally any task that can be measured by the metrics of productivity—output per hour—is a task we want automation to do. In short, productivity is for robots. Humans excel at wasting time, experimenting, playing, creating, and exploring. None of these fare well under the scrutiny of productivity. That is why science and art are so hard to fund. But they are also the foundation of long-term growth.[11]

We find it hard to think straight about productivity anyway. Kelly is comfortable with the idea of robots taking over far more of the work people currently undertake. Some economists have recently, on the contrary, been worried about increasing automation. Paul Krugman waded into the debate, on the heels of the MIT economists Erik Brynjolfsson and Andrew McAfee in their book *Race against the Machine*. Krugman wrote in his *New York Times* column: "What's striking about their examples is that many of the jobs being displaced are high-skill and high-wage; the downside of technology isn't limited to menial workers. Still, can innovation and progress really hurt large numbers of workers, maybe even workers in general? I often encounter assertions that this can't happen. But the truth is that it can, and serious economists have been aware of this possibility for almost two centuries."[12] Indeed, this first happened in the Industrial Revolution, when skilled craft workers were the most disadvantaged by the new looms and mills. So when thinking about the effect on job displacement, we dislike productivity increases.

Yet the "bots" of today are having effects similar to those of the steam-powered mills of the nineteenth century in terms of their disruption to jobs and their impact on the distribution of income. Robots are a new kind of capital equipment, and their spread will reward the owners of this capital initially. Over time, however, each person working will have more capital with which to do their job, just as a weaver could produce more with a mechanical loom than with a hand-loom in his cottage. This translates directly into higher labor productivity and—eventually, and if workers acquire the necessary skills, and society develops the necessary tools for managing income distribution—higher wages. Mechanization or robotization is not new and unusual, no matter how clever and impressive the robots are. They are just the latest generation of capital investment, and it benefits workers to have more capital enhancing what they can do. Eventually, productive investment drives long-run economic growth and the higher incomes that come with that; how the incomes are shared is a social and political challenge. It is, in the long run, a good thing that machines or robots take over activities they can do, freeing humans for the things only they can do. This makes work much more intrinsically rewarding for very many people.

I don't think, however, that we understand how to think about what increasing productivity means, or how its benefits will be shared, when there is no "product." Increased income inequality has accompanied the productivity increases linked to digital technologies, indicating that the gains have not been all that widely shared so far. This accounts for the confusing debate under way among economists about the implications for jobs and incomes, including income distribution, of the current wave of capital investment in digital equipment and machines.

A related issue is how to account for the value of a specific type of intangible product or service, the purely digital items such as online music, search engines, apps, crowd-sourced encyclopedias or software, and so on. Many traditional activities have 'de-materialized,' for instance subscriptions to music or video streaming services rather than buying CDs or

DVDs. Sometimes this simply reflects a change of business model and the new services and prices can (in theory) be measured for GDP. Online markets such as Ebay and Marketplace have enabled secondhand sales to grow; again, measurable in theory but much harder to capture in practice. There is also the so-called 'sharing economy,' where there is a matching service provided (for example by Uber or Airbnb). These involve prices, to the home- or car owner as well as the software platform, but again these might be harder to measure in practice than to identify in theory.

Often, though, digital goods have a price of zero, and with no market price they are not captured fully in GDP statistics. The electricity Google uses will be counted in GDP, and so will the electricity we use to go online, as will ad revenues, and Google salaries. But how would the value of free search figure in the statistics? As Erik Brynjolfsson and Adam Saunders put it, in a nod to the famous statement by Robert Solow about computers, "We see the influence of the information age everywhere, except in the GDP statistics."[13] So, for example, the record industry's sales of music have declined in dollar terms, but there is almost certainly more rather than less listening to music. Some of the revenues have simply moved elsewhere (to streaming services, say), but there is a lot of free listening. The gap between what a consumer pays and the value he or she receives from the purchase is called "consumer surplus," and the growing prevalence of zero-priced goods and services online seems to be increasing consumer surplus.[14] It is another reason to think the wedge between what GDP measures and aggregate economic welfare is growing uncomfortably large. Even worse, the GDP statistics distort the true picture of the economy. For example, the U.S. Bureau of Economic Analysis estimated that consumption of Internet access by Americans *declined* in real terms from the second quarter of 2011 on. This is absurd. Erik Brynjolfsson of MIT has pointed out that the information sector (software, TV and radio, movies, telecommunications, data processing, publishing) accounts for the same share in official GDP figures today as it did twenty-five years ago, at about 4 percent. He and his coauthor JooHee Oh estimate that there has in fact been a gain to consumers averaging about $300 billion a year for a decade from access to free services online, such as Facebook, Wikipedia, Craigslist, and Google.[15] Hal Varian, the chief economist at Google, reckons that free search via Google is worth $150 billion a year to users; of course he would say that, but his calculations seem reasonable. The economist Michael Mandel has estimated that "data" or information needs to be added as a third category to the traditional distinction between goods and services. His adjustment of official U.S. GDP statistics adds 0.6 percentage points to real GDP growth in 2012, a substantial difference—remember that the power of compounding makes seemingly small differences in such numbers large in their effects after a few years.[16]

Official statisticians need to start thinking about how to measure better the production and consumption of "information" or digital products that clearly deliver value to consumers. Because GDP measures only monetary transactions, the new "free" business models are not being well measured, and neither are the new types of activity with zero market price but of great value to consumers. There are very many examples now, from big ones like Wikipedia, YouTube, Twitter, and Facebook, web browsers, search engines, online courses, and so on, to small ones like the countless free blogs. There have always been free but valuable activities, from public libraries to walks in the countryside; the difference now is that nonmonetary activities are extensively intertwined with business, making the concept of the production boundary within which GDP is defined inherently blurred.

SUSTAINABILITY

The third emerging issue for the relevance of GDP—no less tricky than the first two—is that it takes account of the increase in output of goods and services over time without fully accounting for whether or not growth now comes at the expense of growth in the future. GDP statistics do include a measure of the depreciation of physical assets ("capital consumption"), but this is a narrow indicator of how far capital is being used up to consume today by reducing the scope for consumption tomorrow.

One aspect it omits is the need for the physical stock of capital (machines, transportation equipment, buildings) to grow by more than is needed just to make up for depreciation of what is there already. There needs to be additional investment just to keep pace with growth in the population, if consumption per person is to be maintained. This, after all, is what matters, rather than the total size of GDP. This is known in the economics jargon as "capital widening." In addition, if innovation, technical progress, is taken into account, surely it is important to include some indicator of "required" additional investment in the new kinds of capital, to implement the innovation? William Nordhaus and James Tobin put it this way: "This principle [capital widening] is clear enough when growth is simply increase in population and the labor force. Its application to an economy with technological progress is by no means clear. Indeed, the very concept of national income becomes fuzzy. Should the capital widening requirement then be interpreted to mean that capital should keep pace with output and technology, not just with the labor force?"[17] It is an increasingly pressing question in a highly innovative economy. .

The latest international national accounting standard, SNA2008, has tried to address some of these concerns. The United States is the first country seriously to put into practice its suggested improvements, which include counting spending on research and development as investment rather than a business cost, and estimating as well the value of investment in "artistic originals" such as Hollywood movies and music. Preliminary changes in statistical methodology along these lines led to a one-time jump in U.S. GDP of more than 2 percent in 2007, but a bigger increase of 3.4 percent was announced in mid-2013. The SNA2008 handbook explains that "many of these assets, often seen as a hallmark of the 'new economy,' are associated with the establishment of property rights over knowledge in one form or another."

These questions about the treatment of investment in assets are just one dimension of sustainability, however; there are others. More often, the term *sustainability* refers to the extent to which GDP growth from year to year depletes natural resources or harms the environment in other ways. The most important amendment needed to the existing national accounts statistics is to take account of the balance between investment in new assets and the depletion or depreciation of existing assets. Without this, we can know about the current rate of economic growth but have no information about whether it could be sustained in future. The Weitzman/Oulton approach has the advantage of being a reasonably straightforward change to existing statistics. A more thoroughgoing, but also more ambitious and difficult, approach is to develop a measure of "comprehensive wealth"—all of the nation's assets and how they change from year to year—which would give more emphasis to environmental measures, needed for a true indicator of sustainability.[18]

It should be said that official statisticians have been paying increasing attention to environmental measures, ranging from CO_2 emissions and water quality to the extraction of mineral resources. In 2012, the UN Statistical Commission adopted a new international statistical standard with equal status to the System of National Accounts, the System of Environmental Economic Accounting or SEEA. Some countries have been publishing what are known as "satellite accounts" on the environment for a number of years, although it is hard to identify any direct influence they have had on economic policy debates. As long as political contests focus on economic growth, as I think they always will, a set of statistics labeled "satellite" is unlikely to be influential.

Although national statistical offices in many countries have become much more diligent in collecting environmental statistics, and people who are interested or concerned can look them up, most people are not sufficiently interested or adept with the databases. If policy decisions are to take account of the environmental impact of growth, and the extent to which current growth comes at the expense of future growth, natural depreciation also needs to be accounted for in GDP, alongside the depreciation of machines and roads.

Sustainability means that people in successive generations should have what they need to be at least as well off as we are. There are different types of assets to take into account in being able to evaluate whether the current increase in GDP is sustainable or not. One is the obvious measure of physical assets, including infrastructure; this is what "investment" in conventional GDP definitions means—subject to the capital widening issue. Natural assets are another, including obviously valuable resources such as oil deposits but also less obviously valuable ones such as clean air and a stable climate.

A third type of asset is what economists term "human capital," or a development economist might instead label as "capabilities"—in other words, how well equipped is a people to make use of the other assets they have at their disposal? What is their level of education and practical skill, or their ability to create and innovate? Another, and perhaps related, asset is "social capital," a hard-to-define concept that tries to capture how well people are able to organize collectively through political and other institutions to grow the economy. It overlaps with other concepts such as culture. Although it is hard to define and therefore measure, it clearly affects economic growth. To give just one example out of many, former colonies that inherited the English legal framework have grown faster and have higher incomes per head now than those that inherited the French legal framework. Legal traditions would be one of the factors contributing to social capital. Neither kind of investment, in human or social capital, is measured in conventional statistics, although spending on some "inputs," such as education expenditure, will be counted. This is understandable when the concepts are hard to pin down precisely in the first place, but they matter. A country should not regret forgoing some increase in GDP this year for the sake of investments that will contribute to human and/or social capital.

Some governments, although not enough, calculate generational accounts that tell them the cost in the future of their spending policies and whether tax revenues will be adequate, given the age structure of the population. The World Bank has started work on measuring "comprehensive wealth," which includes natural assets, "human capital" (the level of people's skills and abilities), and also physical infrastructure.

An alternative approach, mentioned in chapter 5, is Martin Weitzman's Net National Product, derived from standard GDP and related statistics, which measures the country's maximum sustainable level of consumption.[19] It does not include investment in or depletion of environmental stocks: for example, the U.K. national accounts include mineral oil exploration as part of gross investment but depletion of oil and gas stocks by extraction is not included in depreciation and thus NNP is overstated. But NNP could be amended to take account of this.[20]

Conclusion: What National Statistics Do We Need in the Twenty-first Century?

Public discussion of the economy refers to GDP all the time, and the term has become so familiar that nobody gives it much thought. All the complexities and challenges of constructing the statistics are submerged. It is our shorthand for how well the economy is doing.

Economic growth is essential, for reasons set out in this book. It is one of the key contributors to our well-being, although certainly not the only one. It is for this reason also politically vital. Without economic growth, there would not be enough jobs to keep the unemployment rate down to a tolerable level. It is not possible to redistribute incomes unless the economic pie is growing. Democracy itself is more fragile when growth halts.[21] 'No growth,' desired by some, is for the rich. There is, for now, no alternative to using GDP to measure economic growth.

Of course it is a flawed measure. The later chapters of this book have spelled out some of the flaws, as well as some supplementary or alternative approaches. These include looking at the Human Development Index as a wider indicator, or adopting "dashboards" of indicators, and some suggestions such as conducting regular time-use surveys so we can measure household production and the informal economy, or including depreciation of at least some natural assets such as oil and gas reserves.

Despite such caveats, GDP does a good job of measuring how fast (or not) the output of "the economy" is growing, and GDP growth is closely linked to social welfare. GDP struggles with measuring innovation, quality, and intangibles, but it does a better job than any currently available alternative. There are some alternatives for measuring welfare rather than output, but these two concepts are distinct and should not be muddled up. Some economists are concerned that budget cuts at national statistical offices are making it harder to get national account statistics that are of adequate quality, and they regret the diversion of resources to more fashionable indicators such as "happiness"; they would certainly argue against diluting any further the effort that goes into collecting GDP and its related statistics.

Other reforms are more urgent than asking citizens general questions about their level of well-being. The UN's standard GDP definition should abandon the misleading FISIM construction and revert to a more straightforward approach to measuring the financial sector.

National statistical offices should either do regular time-use surveys so they can monitor the informal economy, or develop other measures of household production. There is no good rationale for ignoring it, and it is no harder to measure than illegal drugs or prostitution.

There is no need to develop new measures of "happiness" or new indicators like the ISEW or GPI (although perhaps in time the approach to "happiness" or "well-being" will become more sophisticated than it is now, and useful for policy). There are already good indicators of welfare and all the components that go into the GDP alternatives. The HDI is a well-understood measure. Variants of the ISEW are flawed because the weights used for the various components are arbitrary, and there is no consensus about them.

A regular, official indicator of sustainability is urgently needed, however. At present, governments have nothing to tell them whether the growth their policies are delivering is coming at the expense of growth and living standards in the future. Comparisons between an individual and a whole nation are never exact (and can indeed be misleading), but just as a business needs to have a balance sheet as well as profit and loss accounts, a nation needs to keep an eye on its assets. A country has the power to influence the quantity and value of its assets in the way a business or household does not. But this is limited, and governments need to ensure that people in the future will be able to enjoy at least as high a living standard as we do now, by watching out for excessive depletion of natural resources or emissions of CO_2, or by making sure the bill future taxpayers will face for pensions and health care does not grow too much.[22] The whole set of national accounts data does contain some information on stocks and assets (or debts) as well as flows of income or expenditure, but it is neither comprehensive nor straightforward to use.

The *collection* of statistics needs to be modernized. National accounts and other official economic data are collected from a range of sources, as discussed in chapter 1, but surveys of individuals and businesses form their backbone. It is almost impossible for the conventional survey methods, involving sending forms to certain businesses or setting researchers to collect information on prices from different outlets, to keep up to date when the structure of the economy changes. To give one obvious example, the spread of shopping either in "big-box" stores or online changes the way price data need to be gathered, as prices are likely to be lower than elsewhere in both cases. The emergence of new sectors of the economy, like digital start-ups or mobile telephony, mean the collection of statistics will lag on their levels of employment and investment. And so on.

It is time to use the new technologies to start collecting data. This could be particularly important in developing countries, where the prevalence of mobile phones now offers an unprecedented opportunity to measure the economy. Just as "user-generated content" used carefully has become an important resource in disaster response, in social enterprises, and in the news media, user-collected statistics could prove a more timely and accurate data source in the future. There seem to be very few trials, however—just a handful collecting health data. National statisticians in the developed economies have perhaps not been best placed to experiment with online or mobile collection of raw data. But it might help reduce their costs, and they would probably get a more dynamic and accurate portrait of economic activity. However, it is hard for cash-strapped official statistical bodies to do this, so one possibility under discussion in their circles is whether they could develop a way of validating statistics collected by others— such as the Billion Prices Project or commercially-provided statistics—and possible giving statistically valid approaches an official seal of approval.[23]

Interesting or important as reforms like these would be, however, there is a deeper question. Has GDP reached its limits because of the changed character of the economy? The definitions involved in the national accounts have become far too convoluted and complicated, and take up too much of the statistics budget—except, of course, in countries such as Greece that used to make up figures, or those African countries that have not collected the necessary raw statistics. The databases of GDP in many countries over decades, used so often by economists to develop theories and policies, lead us to think that GDP is a natural object that we can measure with increasing accuracy. But the accuracy is spurious, and the "object" being measured is only an idea, not something with an independent existence waiting to be discovered and counted.

The U.S. Commerce Department called GDP one of the greatest inventions of the twentieth century, and so it was. There is no replacement for it on the horizon. But rather than continue down the path of making the definitions and refinements ever more complicated, statisticians and economists should think more deeply about what we mean by "the economy" in the twenty-first century.

The structure and character of the economy has changed profoundly as growth has continued over the decades. "GDP mainly measures market production," according to the high-profile Sen-Stiglitz-Fitoussi commission looking at measures "Beyond GDP." This gets it backward: GDP *defines* market production, which is then measured by the official statisticians. But there is no clear definition of "the economy" that would stand for all time, and around which one can measure "satellites" like the environment or housework. Rather, the economy is a fluid concept, which could and probably should be redefined. That will involve reforming GDP substantially or replacing it with a measure, or more likely a series of measures or a dashboard, suited to a new definition of the economy.

Why will a more radical rethinking of "the economy" be required at some point? For reasons like those already set out here. Above all, the economy is not primarily a physical but rather an intangible entity now. It has always been difficult enough to separate money GDP into "quantity" and "price" components, taking account of improvements in quality and choice. This is not a meaningful exercise when quality and personalization are central to the service or aspect of the goods being supplied. Related to this kind of change in the economy, the boundary between paid work in the market and unpaid work has become fuzzier the more people contribute to voluntary value-creation (Wikipedia and Linux being the canonical examples), or draw on their "leisure" activities for their paid work (having a brilliant idea while out with friends), or mingle the two (a landscape gardener practicing new designs on family members before selling them to clients). The financial crisis has given extra urgency to the need to rethink the concept of economic value. In this final chapter, I've set out some important areas to consider, but this is certainly not the last word on what "the economy" consists of today.

Meanwhile, it is above all important not to confuse GDP with social welfare. The way the economy has changed has made the gap between GDP and welfare bigger than it used to be. The acceleration in the variety of products, in customization, and in the blurring of the boundary between leisure and work in many creative professions or vocations—all of these mean that GDP growth increasingly *under*estimates increases in welfare. Contrary to the popular impression that it exaggerates the improvement in our standard of living, the opposite may be true.

At present, we are in a statistical fog, without the information needed about either the negative aspects of growth when it is unsustainable and depletes the natural and other assets available for the future, or the positive aspects, when it delivers innovations and creativity. GDP, for all its flaws, is still a bright light shining through the mist.

ACKNOWLEDGMENTS

This book came about because of the enthusiasm of Peter Dougherty of Princeton University Press for a talk I gave at the think tank Policy Exchange in 2011, and I'm grateful to him for suggesting that I should extend it. I would like to thank the following people for their suggestions and comments on drafts of the book and on the hardback edition: Reuven Brenner, Simon Briscoe, Wendy Carlin, Brett Christophers, Tony Clayton, James Grant, Joe Grice, Bob Hahn, Andrew Haldane, Jonathan Haskel, Harold James, Andrew Kelly, Stephen King, Merijn Knibbe, Rob Metcalfe, James Rakowski, Peter Sinclair, Mark Skousen, Paola Subacchi, Romesh Vaitilingam, and Robert Went. I am grateful to the OECD for hosting a number of discussions on the subject of measuring social welfare. I have also benefited from comments from faculty and students attending a lecture I gave at the University of East Anglia in February 2013, from attendees at a roundtable at the Legatum Institute in June 2012, at a roundtable at the Centre for the Study of Financial Innovation in March 2014, at a seminar at Statistics New Zealand in July 2014, and from readers and reviewers of the first edition.

As ever, I'm immensely grateful to my agent, Sara Menguc, and owe huge thanks to my long-suffering family, Rory, Adam, and Rufus. And to Cabbage the dog, who contributes not at all to GDP but greatly to welfare.

NOTES

INTRODUCTION

1. "Greece's Statistics Chief Faces Criminal Probe," *Financial Times*, 27 November 2011; "Greek Statistics Chief Faces Charges over Claims of Inflated 2009 Deficit Figure," *Ekathimerini.com*, 22 January 2013, http://www.ekathimerini.com/4dcgi/_w_articles_wsite1_1_22/01/2013_479717; "Numbers Game Turns Nasty for Greek Stats Chief," *Reuters*, 14 March 2013, http://uk.reuters.com/article/2013/03/14/uk-greece-stats-insight-id UKBRE92D0AW20130314. Both accessed 15 March 2013.

2. "Report on Greek Government Debt and Deficit Statistics," European Commission, January 2010. By 2008, Greece had become the world's fifth biggest importer of military equipment.

3. See Tim Harford, "Look Out for Number 1," http://timharford.com/2011/09/look-out-for-no-1/; Andrew McCullogh, "Beware of Greeks Bearing Stats," *Significance*, http://www.significancemagazine.org/details/webexclusive/1406899/Beware-of-Greeks-bearing-stats-Debt-statistics-and-Benfords-Law.html; and "The Curious Case of Benford's Law," *WolframAlpha Blog*, 13 December 2010, http://blog.wolframalpha.com/2010/12/13/the-curious-case-of-benfords-law/. Benford's Law applies to many types of data where the entries span several orders of magnitude from units and tens to millions and billions, not just economic statistics. Belgium's data also fail to conform, whereas statistics from Italy, Portugal, and Spain satisfy the law.

4. J. Steven Landefeld, "GDP: One of the Great Inventions of the 20th Century," in Bureau of Economic Analysis, *Survey of Current Business*, January 2000, http://www.bea.gov/scb/account_articles/general/0100od/maintext.htm.

CHAPTER 1: FROM THE EIGHTEENTH CENTURY TO THE 1930S: WAR AND DEPRESSION

1. Frits Bos, "Uses of National Accounts: History, International Standardization and Applications in the Netherlands," MPRA Paper no. 9387, 30 June 2008, http://mpra.ub.uni-muenchen.de/9387/. Accessed 1 August 2012.

2. Benjamin H. Mitra-Kahn, "Redefining the Economy: How the 'Economy' Was Invented, 1620" (Ph.D. dissertation, City University London, 2011), http://openaccess.city.ac.uk/1276/. Accessed 3 August 2012.

3. Adam Smith, *The Wealth of Nations* (first published 1776), book II, chap. 3.

4. Geoff Tily, "John Maynard Keynes and the Development of National Accounts in Britain, 1895–1941," *Review of Income and Wealth* 55, no. 2 (2009): 331–359.

5. Angus Maddison, *The World Economy: Historical Statistics* (Paris: Organization for Economic Cooperation and Development, 2003), preface.

6. Joined by the United States after the attack on Pearl Harbor in December 1941.

7. See Robert William Fogel, Enid M. Fogel, Mark Guglielmo, and Nathaniel Grotte, *Political Arithmetic: Simon Kuznets and the Empirical Tradition in Economics* (Chicago: University of Chicago Press, 2013).

8. Jim Lacey, *Keep from All Thoughtful Men: How US Economists Won World War II* (Annapolis: Naval Institute Press, 2011), 43.

9. Cited in Mitra-Kahn, "Redefining the Economy."

10. Richard Stone, *The Role of Measurement in Economics* (Cambridge: Cambridge University Press, 1951), 43.

11. Carol S. Carson, "The History of the United States National Income and Product Accounts: The Development of an Analytical Tool," *Review of Income and Wealth* 21 (1975): 153–181.

12. Lacey, *Keep from All Thoughtful Men*, 47.

13. Richard Kane, "Measures and Motivations: U.S. National Income and Product Estimates during the Great Depression and World War II," Munich Working Paper, February 2012, http://mpra.ub.uni-muenchen.de/44336/. Accessed 27 March 2013.

14. J. M. Keynes, *How to Pay for the War* (first pub. 1940), reprinted in *Essays in Persuasion* (Basingstoke: Macmillan for the Royal Economic Society, 1989).

15. Quoted in J. Steven Landefeld, "GDP: One of the Great Inventions of the 20th Century," in Bureau of Economic Analysis, *Survey of Current Business*, January 2000, http://www.bea.gov/scb/account_articles/general/0100od/maintext.htm.

16. http://www.oecd.org/general/themarshallplanspeechatharvarduniversity5june1947.htm. Accessed 21 January 2013.

17. Twenty-three billion in 1952 dollars. See Stephen Lewarne and David Snelbecker, "Economic Governance in War Torn Economies: Lessons Learned from the Marshall Plan to the Reconstruction of Iraq," USAID report, December 2004, http://www.oecd.org/derec/unitedstates/36144028.pdf. Accessed 21 January 2013.

18. Now part of Global Insight, http://www.ihs.com/products/global -insight/index.aspx?pu=1&rd=globalinsight_com. I worked for DRI's London office for two years in the late 1980s, as an economic forecaster.

19. Olivier Blanchard and Daniel Leigh, "Growth Forecast Errors and Fiscal Multipliers," IMF Working Paper 13/1, January 2013, http://www .imf.org/external/pubs/ft/wp/2013/wp1301.pdf. Accessed 15 January 2013. See also G. Corsetti, "What Determines Government Spending Multipliers," IMF Working Paper, 2012, http://www.imf.org/external/pubs/ft/wp/2012/ wp12150.pdf. Accessed 28 March 2013.

20. Stone, *The Role of Measurement in Economics*, 9.

21. François Lequiller and Derek Blades, *Understanding National Accounts* (Paris: Organization for Economic Cooperation and Development, 2006).

22. Good introductions to the detail are J. Steven Landefeld, Eugene P. Seskin, and Barbara M. Fraumeni, "Taking the Pulse of the Economy: Measuring GDP," *Journal of Economic Perspectives* 22, no. 2 (2008): 193–216; Carlos M. Gutierrez et al., "Measuring the Economy: A Primer on GDP and the National Income and Product Accounts," Bureau of Economic Analysis, U.S. Department of Commerce, September 2007, http://www .bea.gov/national/pdf/nipa_primer.pdf; and Lequiller and Blades, *Understanding National Accounts*.

23. Landefeld et al., "Taking the Pulse of the Economy."

24. There is increasing interest in Gross Output as a measure of the economy, without deducting intermediate goods, and the US Bureau of Economic Analysis has recently started to publish this quarterly. Its advocates see it as a better indicator of production or the supply-side of the economy, and argue that this is more important than the demand-side focus that results from looking at GDP defined in terms of the sum of different categories of expenditure. See Mark Skousen, "At Last, a Better Economic Measure," Wall Street Journal, 22 April 2014.

25. Wikipedia lists the main formulas: http://en.wikipedia.org/wiki/ List_of_price_index_formulas.

26. Xan Rice, "Nigeria Statistics Chief Has Almost Figured Out the Economy," *Financial Times*, 22 May 2013.

27. http://paris21.org/nsds-status. Accessed 7 January 2013.

28. Alwyn Young, "The African Growth Miracle," LSE Working Paper, 2009, http://eprints.lse.ac.uk/33928/.

29. http://www.huffingtonpost.com/marcelo-giugale/fix-africas -statistics_b_2324936.html, 18 December 2012. Accessed 7 January 2013. See also Morten Jerven, *Poor Numbers: How We Are Misled by African Development Statistics and What to Do about It* (Ithaca: Cornell University Press, 2013).

30. Young, "The African Growth Miracle."

31. Maddison, *The World Economy*, 79.

32. "Toward a More Accurate Measure of the Cost of Living," 4 December 1996, http://www.ssa.gov/history/reports/boskinrpt.html. Accessed 15 January 2013. See also Robert J. Gordon, "The Boskin Commission Report and Its Aftermath," http://faculty-web.at.northwestern.edu/economics/gordon/346.html. Accessed 15 January 2013.

33. Quoted in *The Guardian*, 3 December 2006, http://www.guardian.co.uk/business/2006/dec/03/past.interviews. Accessed 28 March 2013.

34. Lequiller and Blades, *Understanding National Accounts*, 98.

CHAPTER 2: 1945 TO 1975: THE GOLDEN AGE

1. J. M. Keynes, *Economic Consequences of the Peace* (New York: Harcourt, Brace and Howe, 1920), chapter 6.

2. All these growth figures are from Angus Maddison, *The World Economy: A Millennial Perspective* (Paris: Organization for Economic Cooperation and Development, 2000).

3. Reuven Brenner argues for the importance of democratic institutions over aid for the post-war revival in Europe, and believes Marshall Aid was far less important than I suggest here. See Reuven Brenner, *Labyrinths of Prosperity: Economic Follies, Democratic Remedies* (Ann Arbor: University of Michigan Press, 1994).

4. F. Janossy, *The End of the Economic Miracle* (White Plains, NY: International Arts and Sciences Press, 1969).

5. Brilliantly evoked in Francis Spufford, *Red Plenty* (London: Faber, 2010).

6. Frits Bos "Uses of National Accounts: History, International Standardization and Applications in the Netherlands," MPRA Paper no. 9387, 30 June 2008, http://mpra.ub.uni-muenchen.de/9387/, 29. Accessed 1 August 2012.

7. Nicholas Oulton, "The Wealth and Poverty of Nations: True PPPs for 141 Countries," Centre for Economic Performance, London School of Economics, March 2010.

8. Robert H. Wade, "Is Globalization Reducing Poverty and Inequality?" *World Development* 32, no. 4 (2004): 567–589.

9. Ibid.

10. Surjut Bhalla, "World Bank—Peddling Poverty," *Business Standard*, 22 December 2007, http://www.business-standard.com/article/opinion/surjit-s-bhalla-world-bank-peddling-poverty-107122201086_1.html. Accessed 23 March 2013.

11. Oulton, "The Wealth and Poverty of Nations."

CHAPTER 3: THE LEGACY OF THE 1970S:
A CRISIS OF CAPITALISM

1. Real GDP per capita, Western Europe and the United States, in 1990 adjusted dollars, from Angus Maddison, *The World Economy: A Millennial Perspective* (Paris: Organization for Economic Cooperation and Development, 2000).

2. "A Woman Complains," *Business Week*, 3 October 1942, http://invention.smithsonian.org/centerpieces/whole_cloth/u7sf/u7images/act4/complains.html. Accessed 21 January 2013.

3. Siddhartha Mukherjee, *The Emperor of All Maladies* (London: Fourth Estate, 2011), 21–22.

4. David Landes, *The Wealth and Poverty of Nations* (New York: W. W. Norton, 1998).

5. A. W. Phillips, "The Relationship between Unemployment and the Rate of Change of Money Wages in the United Kingdom 1861–1957," *Economica* 25, no. 100 (1958): 283–299.

6. Later the "non-accelerating inflation rate of unemployment" or NAIRU. Macroeconomic textbooks cover this. See, for example, Wendy Carlin and David Soskice, *Macroeconomics: Imperfections, Institutions and Policies* (Oxford: Oxford University Press, 2005).

7. International Monetary Fund, World Bank, Organization for Economic Cooperation and Development, and the European Bank for Reconstruction and Development, *A Study of the Soviet Economy* (Paris: Organization for Economic Cooperation and Development, 1991).

8. J. A. Piazza, "Globalization Quiescence: Globalization, Union Density and Strikes in 15 Industrialized Countries," *Economic and Industrial Democracy* 26, no. 2 (2005): 289–314.

9. Amartya Sen, *Poverty and Famines: An Essay on Entitlements and Deprivation* (Oxford: Clarendon Press, 1982).

10. Amartya Sen, *Development as Freedom* (Oxford: Oxford University Press, 1999).

11. See these and other examples in Charles Kenny, *Getting Better* (New York: Basic Books, 2011).

CHAPTER 4: 1995 TO 2005: THE NEW PARADIGM

1. Paul A. David, 1990. "The Dynamo and the Computer: An Historical Perspective on a Modern Productivity Problem," *American Economic Review* 80, no. 2 (1990): 355–361. Available at http://elsa

.berkeley.edu/~bhhall/e124/David90_dynamo.pdf. Accessed 23 January 2013.

2. Angus Maddison, *The World Economy: A Millennial Perspective* (Paris: Organization for Economic Cooperation and Development, 1999).

3. Tim Berners-Lee's message at the opening ceremony of the 2012 London Olympic Games.

4. Robert Solow, "We'd Better Watch Out," *New York Times Book Review*, 12 July 1987, 36.

5. Bill Lewis et al., "US Productivity Growth, 1995–2000," McKinsey Global Institute, October 2001, http://www.mckinsey.com/insights/americas/us_productivity_growth_1995-2000.

6. Erik Brynjolfsson and Lorin M. Hitt, "Beyond Computation: Information Technology, Organizational Transformation and Business Performance," *Journal of Economic Perspectives* 14, no. 4 (2000): 23–48.

7. Robert J. Gordon, "Is US Economic Growth Over? Faltering Innovation Confronts the Six Headwinds," CEPR Policy Insight no. 63, 2012, http://www.cepr.org/pubs/PolicyInsights/CEPR_Policy_Insight_063.asp.

8. Alan Greenspan, *The Age of Turbulence* (New York: Allen Lane, 2007), 167.

9. For a survey of the debate, see Coen Teulings and Richard Baldwin, eds., *Secular Stagnation: Facts, Causes and Cures* (London: CEPR 2014).

10. S. Broadberry, "Britain's 20th Century Productivity Performance," Warwick University working paper, 2005, http://www2.warwick.ac.uk/fac/soc/economics/staff/academic/broadberry/wp/labmkt5.pdf. Accessed 23 January 2013.

11. J. Bradford DeLong, "How Fast Is Modern Economic Growth?" http://www.j-bradford-delong.net/Comments/FRBSF_June11.html, citing William D. Nordhaus, "Do Real-Output and Real-Wage Measures Capture Reality? The Price of Light Suggests Not," Cowles Foundation Discussion Paper 1078, September 1994, http://cowles.econ.yale.edu/P/cp/p09b/p0957.pdf. Accessed 23 January 2013.

12. Jerry A. Hausman, "Valuation of New Goods under Perfect and Imperfect Competition," NBER Working Paper no. 4970, December 1994.

13. William D. Nordhaus, "The Progress of Computing," Department of Economics, Yale University, August 2001.

14. William J. Baumol, *The Free-Market Innovation Machine* (Princeton, NJ: Princeton University Press, 2002).

15. Mark Bils and Peter J. Klenow, "The Acceleration in Variety Growth," *American Economic Review* 91, no. 2 (2001): 274–280.

16. Diane Coyle, *The Weightless World* (Oxford: Capstone, 1996).

CHAPTER 5: OUR TIMES: THE GREAT CRASH

1. James Glassman and Kevin Hassett, *Dow 36,000* (New York: Three Rivers Press, 1999).

2. Robert Shiller, *Irrational Exuberance* (Princeton, NJ: Princeton University Press, 2000).

3. See John Kay, *Obliquity* (London: Profile Books, 2010).

4. Kenneth Pomeranz, *The Great Divergence: China, Europe, and the Making of the Modern World Economy* (Princeton, NJ: Princeton University Press, 2000).

5. "Has China Already Passed the U.S. as the World's Largest Economy?" *WashintonBlog*, 5 April 2012, http://www.washingtonsblog.com/2012/04/has-china-already-passed-the-u-s-as-the-worlds-largest-economy.html.

6. Andrew Haldane, "The $100 Billion Question," speech, March 2010, http://www.bankofengland.co.uk/publications/Pages/news/2010/036.aspx. Accessed 3 August 2012.

7. Andrew Haldane, Simon Brennan, and Vasilcios Madouros, "The Contribution of the Financial Sector: Miracle or Mirage?" in *The Future of Finance: The LSE Report* (London: London School of Economics and Political Science, 2010), 87–120, http://harr123et.files.wordpress.com/2010/07/futureoffinance5.pdf.

8. Gross value added less compensation for employees and other taxes on production.

9. François Lequiller and Derek Blades, *Understanding National Accounts* (Paris: Organization for Economic Cooperation and Development, 2006).

10. A further complication is that financial services represent intermediate consumption by other businesses and households, but there is no obvious way to allocate the amount between the two categories.

11. Haldane et al., "The Contribution of the Financial Sector."

12. Susanto Basu, Robert Inklaar, and J. Christina Wang, "The Value of Risk: Measuring the Services of U.S. Commercial Banks," *Economic Inquiry* 49, no. 1 (2011): 226–245.

13. Antonio Colangelo and Robert Inklaar, "Banking Sector Output Measurement in the Euro Area: A Modified Approach," ECB Working Paper Series no. 1204, 2010.

14. For an example of this lobbying, see Haley Sweetland Edwards, "He Who Makes the Rules," *Washington Monthly*, March 2013, http://www.washingtonmonthly.com/magazine/march_april_2013/features/he_who_makes_the_rules043315.php?page=all.

15. Alastair Darling, *Back from the Brink: 1,000 Days at Number 11* (London: Atlantic Books, 2011).

16. Alan Greenspan, "Dodd-Frank Fails to Meet Test of Our Times," *FinancialTimes*, 29 March 2011, http://www.ft.com/cms/s/0/14662fd8-5a28 -11e0-86d3-00144feab49a.html#axzz1HtbBWxDD. Accessed 27 March 2013.

17. Brett Christophers, *Banking across Boundaries: Placing Finance in Capitalism* (Chichester, West Sussex: Wiley-Blackwell, 2013), 143.

18. Ibid., 192.

19. Leonidas Akritidis, "Improving the Measurement of Banking Services in the UK National Accounts," *Economic and Labour Market Review* 1, no. 5 (May 2007): 29–37.

20. Christophers, *Banking across Boundaries*, 239.

21. Richard Stone, "The Accounts of Society," Nobel Memorial Lecture, 8 December 1984, http://www.nobelprize.org/nobel_prizes/economic -sciences/laureates/1984/stone-lecture.pdf.

22. Christophers, *Banking across Boundaries*, 105.

23. The canonical books are Tim Jackson, *Prosperity without Growth: Economics for a Finite Planet* (London: Routledge, 2009); and Paul R. Ehrlich, *The Population Bomb* (New York: Ballantine, 1968).

24. Clyde Haberman, "For Italy's Entrepreneurs, the Figures Are Bella," *New York Times*, 16 July 1989, http://www.nytimes.com/1989/07/16/ magazine/for-italy-s-entrepreneurs-the-figures-are-bella.html?page wanted=all&src=pm.

25. Friedrich Schneider, "Size and Development of the Shadow Economy of 31 European and 5 Other OECD Countries from 2003 to 2012: Some New Facts," Johannes Kepler University, December 2011, http:// www.econ.jku.at/members/Schneider/files/publications/2012/ShadEc Europe31.pdf. See also Friedrich Schneider with Dominik Enste, "Hiding in the Shadows: The Growth of the Underground Economy," International Monetary Fund, March 2002, http://www.imf.org/external/pubs/ft/issues/ issues30/index.htm#3.

26. http://www-2009.timeuse.org/information/studies/.

27. Jonathan Gershuny, "Time-Use Surveys and the Measurement of National Well-Being," Centre for Time-Use Research, Department of Sociology, University of Oxford, September 2011, http://www.ons.gov.uk/ons/ rel/environmental/time-use-surveys-and-the-measurement-of-national -well-being/article-by-jonathan-gershuny/index.html.

28. Quoted in *The Observer*, 24 March 2013, http://www.guardian. co.uk/money/2013/mar/24/poorer-familes-deserve-childcare. Accessed 27 March 2013.

29. Michael Sandel, "What Money Can't Buy: The Moral Limits of Markets," Tanner Lectures on Human Values, delivered at Brasenose College, Oxford, 1998.

30. See Diane Coyle, *The Economics of Enough* (Princeton, NJ: Princeton University Press, 2011).

31. For details, see http://www.ons.gov.uk/ons/guide-method/user-guidance/well-being/index.html.

32. David G. Blanchflower and Andrew G. Oswald, "Is Well-being U-Shaped over the Life Cycle?" *Social Science and Medicine* 66, no. 8 (2008): 1733–1749.

33. William D. Nordhaus and James Tobin, "Is Growth Obsolete?" in *Economic Research: Retrospect and Prospect*, vol. 5, *Economic Growth*, ed. William D. Nordhaus and James Tobin (New York: National Bureau of Economic Research, 1972), http://www.nber.org/books/nord72-1.

34. Simon Kuznets, *National Income and Capital Formation, 1919–1935* (New York: National Bureau of Economic Research, 1937), 37.

35. Nordhaus and Tobin, "Is Growth Obsolete?"

36. http://www.foe.co.uk/community/tools/isew/make-own.html.

37. J. Bradford DeLong, "How Fast Is Modern Economic Growth?" http://www.j-bradford-delong.net/Comments/FRBSF_June11.html. Accessed 12 July 2013.

38. Nicholas Oulton, "Hooray for GDP!" Centre for Economic Performance, London School of Economics, June 2012, paper submitted to the LSE Growth Commission.

39. *Report of the Commission on the Measurement of Economic Performance and Social Progress*, available at http://www.stiglitz-sen-fitoussi.fr/en/index.htm. Accessed 23 January 2013.

Chapter 6: The Future: Twenty-first-Century GDP

1. "The Right Stuff: America's Move to Mass Customization," *Federal Reserve Bank of Dallas 1998 Annual Report*, http://www.dallasfed.org/assets/documents/fed/annual/1999/ar98.pdf.

2. Ibid.

3. See Amartya Sen, *Development as Freedom* (Oxford: Oxford University Press, 2001).

4. "The Right Stuff."

5. For a study of the surprising complexity of even a simple product, see Pietra Rivoli, *Travels of a T-shirt in the Global Economy* (Hoboken, NJ: Wiley, 2005).

6. Susan N. Houseman and Kenneth F. Ryder, ed., *Measurement Issues Arising from the Growth of Globalization: Conference Papers*, Upjohn Institute, 2010, http://www.bea.gov/papers/pdf/bea_2010_conference%20papers_final.pdf.

7. Yuqing Xing, "How the iPhone Widens the US Trade Deficit with China," *Vox*, 10 April 2011, http://www.voxeu.org/index.php?q=node/6335. Accessed 14 January 2013.

8. Andrew Walker, "UK Productivity Puzzle Baffles Economists," *BBC World Service*, 17 October 2012, http://www.bbc.co.uk/news/business-19981498.

9. Diane Coyle, *The Weightless World* (Oxford: Capstone, 1996).

10. W. J. Baumol and W. G. Bowen, "On the Performing Arts: The Anatomy of Their Economic Problems," *American Economic Review* 55, no. 1/2 (1965): 495–502.

11. Kevin Kelly, "The Post-Productive Economy," *The Technium*, 1 January 2013, http://www.kk.org/thetechnium/archives/2013/01/the_post-produc.php.

12. Paul Krugman, "Robots and Robber Barons," *New York Times*, 9 December 2012, http://www.nytimes.com/2012/12/10/opinion/krugman-robots-and-robber-barons.html?_r=0.

13. Erik Brynjolfsson and Adam Saunders, "What the GDP Gets Wrong," *MIT Sloan Management Review*, fall 2009, http://sloanreview.mit.edu/article/what-the-gdp-gets-wrong-why-managers-should-care/. Accessed 27 March 2013.

14. See, for example, "What Good Is the Internet?" *Economist*, 8 March 2013, http://www.economist.com/blogs/freeexchange/2013/03/technology. Accessed 27 March 2013.

15. Erik Brynjolfsson and JooHee Oh, "The Attention Economy: Measuring the Value of Free Digital Services on the Internet," MIT working paper, July 2012. See also a summary in "Net Benefits," *The Economist*, 9 March 2013, http://www.economist.com/news/finance-and-economics/21573091-how-quantify-gains-internet-has-brought-consumers-net-benefits.

16. Michael Mandel, "Beyond Goods and Services: The (Unmeasured) Rise of the Data-Driven Economy," Progressive Policy Institute Policy Memo, October 2012.

17. William D. Nordhaus and James Tobin, "Is Growth Obsolete?" in *Economic Research: Retrospect and Prospect*, vol. 5, *Economic Growth*, ed. William D. Nordhaus and James Tobin (New York: National Bureau of Economic Research, 1972), http://www.nber.org/books/nord72-1.

18. Diane Coyle, *The Economics of Enough* (Princeton, NJ: Princeton University Press, 2011).

19. Martin L. Weitzman, "On the Welfare Significance of National Product in a Dynamic Economy," *Quarterly Journal of Economics* 90 (1976): 156–162; Martin L. Weitzman, *Income, Capital, and the Maximum Principle* (Cambridge, MA: Harvard University Press, 2003).

20. Nicholas Oulton, "The Wealth and Poverty of Nations: True PPPs for 141 Countries," Centre for Economic Performance, London School of Economics, March 2010.

21. Ben Friedman, *The Moral Consequences of Economic Growth* (New York: Alfred A Knopf, 2005).

22. I discussed these issues in more detail in *The Economics of Enough*.

23. See http://bpp.mit.edu/.

INDEX

Note: Figures and tables are indicated by "f" or "t" following page numbers.